THE
FIRST PRINCIPLES

Unlock Your Unstoppable Leadership

THOMAS S. NAROFSKY

Copyright © 2015 THOMAS S. NAROFSKY
All rights reserved.

The Narofsky Consulting Group is committed to building leaders that are ready to lead in an uncertain and ambiguous world with integrity, values, and character.

NarofskyConsultingGroup@gmail.com

Cover design by KJ Paperie
All rights reserved

Disclaimer: There is no official endorsement of this book or the material contained herein by the Department of Defense, United States Strategic Command, or the United States Air Force. The thoughts, opinions, anecdotes, Inspire or Retire Theorem, the F(X) Leadership concepts, the F(X) FORGE Process, the 6P and 8P Focus, the Unstoppable Discovery Process and Life Models, and the First Principles Leadership Models are the intellectual property of the Narofsky Consulting Group. The processes and models contained herein may not be suitable for every situation.

ISBN-13: 978-1505664959
ISBN-10: 1505664950

ACKNOWLEDGEMENT

Leadership is a vast and diverse subject and impossible to write about in just one book. This book does not try to capture everything you need to know about leadership, that would be a foolish endeavor. Instead, this book is based on the principles I used to become a leader in the U.S. Air Force and reach the pinnacle of my career.

It was not my intent to reduce leadership to a set of principles, rules, or precepts that one can follow to always achieve great success by as a leader. By its very nature, leadership is multifaceted, multidimensional, and complex. I chose those aspects of leadership that I have achieved success with and presented them as The First Principles. There are many principles and tenets on which to base a leadership philosophy and strategy.

My philosophy is based on the First Principles presented in the book. I have always viewed leadership as an Art and a Science. An object of beauty and an object of mechanics that must be studied, learned, and experienced. However, the true essence of Unstoppable Leadership is not about organizational processes, office politics, or your position; it is about the people you lead, motivate, and inspire.

DEDICATION

This book is dedicated to my immediate and extended family. There is nothing more precious than the love of your family and I have been blessed with parents that expressed their love daily and encouraged us to reach for the stars.

Special thanks goes to Karis and Joshua of KJ Paperie for designing all my book covers.

This book would not be possible without the love and support of my wife, Dorene. Her patience, support, and understanding over the last three years during my obsession with writing and publishing three books is amazing.

Finally, I am thankful to my Lord, Jesus Christ, for his saving Grace and strength each day. It is through him that I am Unstoppable. (Philippians 4:13)

CONTENTS

	Introduction	Pg. i
1	The Ownership Principle	Pg. 1
2	The Awareness Principle	Pg. 32
3	The Authenticity Principle	Pg. 58
4	The Courage Principle	Pg. 93
5	The Focus Principle	Pg. 114
6	The Adaptability Principle	Pg. 139
7	The Growth Principle	Pg. 171
8	The Alignment Principle	Pg. 211
9	The People Principle	Pg. 239
	Conclusion	Pg. 258

INTRODUCTION

"Leadership is leaders acting - as well as caring, inspiring and persuading others to act -- for certain shared goals that represent the values -- the wants and needs, the aspirations and expectations - of themselves and the people they represent."
James MacGregor Burns

Take a moment and turn on the news, read the newspaper, or check the internet and the conclusion you draw is that we are experiencing a Global Leadership Character Crisis. A crisis of leaders compromising their character at the altar of expedience, personal gain, and likeability. A crisis of leaders devaluing their integrity for duplicitousness, greed, and profit.

Integrity does not seem to be a valuable characteristic in leadership today. It does not seem to matter where you turn, there is another leader falling from grace because they have compromised their personal integrity, their values, and they have sacrificed their character.

Institutions and leaders that should be and were held in high regard--governments, presidents, governors, politicians, CEOs, and military leaders--are guilty of dishonesty, greed, corruption, and self-indulgence. It all stems from a devaluation of personal and leadership integrity and a willingness to compromise character for personal gain.

This devaluation of integrity and a willingness to compromise character for gain can have worldwide implications. In this globally interconnected, ambiguous, and complex world we live in, the single actions of these corrupt institutions and individuals can have massive impact and even worldwide implications.

Their single-minded actions can cause the collapse of organizations, national credit ratings, or worldwide market down turns. Worse yet, their single-mindedness could create a generation of like-minded creatures who end up replacing them as leaders in their organizations.

This new creature, who will be called a leader, will create their own havoc and chaos resulting in leaders who are far worse than those who lead today. There is a serious void of leaders who will lead with integrity and uncompromised character. Why do we have this crisis in the first place? **Bottom Line: We have forgotten that trust, integrity, and character lie at the very core of true leadership.**

We no longer hold these institutions and individuals in high regard and we have become apathetic to their actions. We no longer hold them accountable or responsible for their transgression. We have allowed ourselves to become the frog in the boiling kettle. It is as if we expect it and don't care anymore. We have become numb to the actions of our leaders.

The real problem we have today is that news outlets, celebrities, and politicians are trying to tell us what true leadership should be. We have allowed integrity, accountability, responsibility, trustworthiness, reliability, and credibility to lose their true meanings. It is time for this madness to stop!

It is time we demanded more from our leaders! We need a new breed of leader who not only understands integrity and character, but also lives it daily.

- We need leaders who live their values, their beliefs, and their worldview every day

- We need leaders who believe in integrity, character, competence, courage, and commitment

- We need leaders who value people over profit

- We need leaders who build and develop other leaders of character and integrity instead of creatures of profit and greed

- We need leaders who lead by example and lead with a servant's heart

- We need leaders who are focused purposefully on developing a generation of leaders who are concerned with others more than themselves

- We need leaders who choose to be the very best leader they can be each day and every day; we need leaders who inspire; we need leaders with honor and integrity!

THE INFLUENCE OF LEADERSHIP

Leadership influences and shapes everything in life and in business. Leadership is fundamental to everything we do in life--from leading ourselves, to leading others, to leading in an organization--leadership is everywhere. It does not matter if you are on a battlefield, playing field, boardroom, or back office, leadership matters and makes a difference.

The world around us has changed dramatically and radically with financial market globalization, disruptive technological innovations, and social and information media domination. In this complex, unpredictable, and uncertain world, the importance of personal and professional leadership is undeniable.

Leadership is one of the most desirable and key fundamentals for achieving greatness in effective teams and organizations. In addition, leadership is the essential component for enduring and continuous success in the global marketplace. Leadership is an indispensable component of life. It is the difference between a great life and a life unlived. It is easy to understand and recognize, but difficult to grasp.

THE JOURNEY CONTINUES
"A Journey of a thousand miles begins with one step."
Laozi

The journey to write my first book, *F(X) Leadership: The Art and Science of Leadership,* started on March 22, 2005. How can I be sure of that date? Two reasons-- one, it was my birthday, and two, it was the day I had the opportunity to spend with author Donald T. Phillips who wrote *Lincoln on Leadership*, *The Founding Fathers on Leadership*, and other leadership books.

During his visit we discussed the Airmen's Time program, the Leadership Based Outcomes/Mindset model, the F(X) models, and my Inspire or Retire Theorem which were developed and implemented for the development of our emerging and enduring leaders.

At the end of the day Mr. Phillips pulled me aside and suggested I document what we were doing and to later publish the results in a paper or in a book. That journey lasted eight years and finally the first book was published in 2013.

My first book describes the leadership development project that I developed and the opportunity to lead an amazing team of professionals who implemented it. In the course of the project I applied and refined my F(X) leadership concepts to grow and develop emerging and enduring leaders.

Because of the amount of writing, research, and personal reflection that went into the writing of the first book, I finished my second book a year later.

The genesis of the second book, *You Are Unstoppable: Unleash Your Inspired Life*, was a result of my wounded warrior visits to Brooks Army Medical Center (BAMC) in 2006 prior to my yearlong deployment to the Middle East. What one young Soldier said during my visit made a lasting impact on me and gave me insight about resilience, perseverance, and passion for life. His story of perseverance, positive outlook, and determined resiliency inspired me then and continues to inspire me today.

Despite his life changing injuries, he changed his life and his outlook on life. He chose to live each day intentionally and to its fullest! My second book was a further refinement of my self-development principles, development processes, and the development of the Unstoppable Personal Development Model.

Since 1998, I have served in several military, non-profit, academic, and professional organizations in the capacity of an executive leadership consultant, as well as a human capital strategist reporting to the CEO and the Board of Directors. My role as the executive leadership consultant focused on the growth and development of the people inside the organization.

In my travels to visit local and worldwide organizations, I had the opportunity to travel to 32 different countries and to all 50 States. I had the opportunity to talk with junior employees and CEOs about what we need in future leaders.

The one message that resonated with me during each visit was the need for real and authentic leadership. People want real and genuine leaders who guide, coach, and inspire them.

They want inspiring leaders who create a motivating vision, give a sense of higher purpose, and set a course for personal and professional achievement. They want leaders who lead by serving, believe in more than themselves, and who will stand in the gap and answer the call when required. This plea for real leaders and authentic leadership is happening in society as a whole and throughout the world. People are tired of fake and inauthentic leaders.

THE FIRST PRINCIPLES

The First Principles is not a leadership development book as much as it is recognition of leadership qualities needed to lead today and in the future. It is recognition of the need to inspire people with authentic and genuine leadership while anticipating global trends at the speed and pace of change.

The First Principles listed in this book can stand alone as separate but powerful leadership fundamentals; but, when combined together, they produce a powerful leadership strategy. *The First Principles* is designed for you to reflect on the essential elements of leadership. They are a starting point for you to review and reflect on your own leadership style.

The First Principles is not designed to narrow your scope of leadership, but to expand your thoughts about being a leader. I am not trying to put leadership into box or into a quantifiable list of traits or characteristics, but into ideas and concepts to think about.

In a global, interconnected, and uncertain world the ability to adapt and flex as a leader is to know and understand many elements of leadership, know when to apply them, and then practice the skills. Leaders who do not take the time to reflect and review their skills as a leader fail themselves and their team.

In order to lead effectively you need to know your first principles or your self-evident truths of leadership. Once you know your First Principles, you create an unshakable leadership foundation.

ART AND SCIENCE

Today, leaders have to deal with more complexities, uncertainties, and challenges in a fast-paced, chaotic, dynamic, and ever-changing world. Leadership is both an Art and a Science.

It is a thing of beauty when done right and an object of measured calculations and theories. Leadership requires an understanding of inspiration, ingenuity, design, and discipline.

Leaders must understand both the Art and the Science of leadership. It is a delicate balancing act between the soft arts and the hard sciences of leadership. Both are required to lead effectively and passionately in the complexity and ambiguity of the world.

Although you can read about how important the soft arts of leadership are through textbooks and articles, the true essence is gained from experience and learned through trial and error. They are the true art of leadership because they are learned through experience versus education.

The soft arts of leadership are empathy, emotional intelligence, relationship building, coaching, mentoring, ability to share, inspiring vision, foresight, collaboration, intuition, positive and optimistic attitude, innovation, communication, culture creator, change catalyst, and legacy builder.

The hard sciences of leadership are more educational based and some may even call it management, but the hard sciences are critically important in a complex and uncertain world.

The hard sciences of leadership are divergent and convergent thinking, single-loop and double-loop learning, behavioral science, psychology, sociology, organizational change, decision-making, ability to see and make sense of global trends, business analytics, ability to see and predict shifts in global markets, ability to manage change, and ability to work with diverse people and cultures.

Becoming an Unstoppable Leader is built on the foundation of my First Principles. Being an Unstoppable Leader is challenging because you are holding yourself accountable and responsible to a standard.

As you read each chapter, reflect and consume each principle in this book. Take the time to see how each applies to your life and how you can use them in your daily leadership. This book is for you to think, mull, and reflect on the First Principles.

LEADERSHIP BEGINS WITH YOU

Becoming an Unstoppable Leader begins with you. It begins with a condition of your heart and starts with the desire and passion to make a difference. Leadership encompasses the integration of the heart, mind, body, and soul.

Unstoppable Leadership is a commitment to lead in a different way--it is a lifestyle, not just a role you play. It begins when you start leading yourself, establishing a vision for your life, and setting goals to achieve. As your personal leadership matures, you move into leading others with the goal of accomplishing goals and developing your people. As your leadership skills grow, develop, and mature, you begin to lead teams and finally, organizations.

It all begins with your transformational choice to be a self-leader and lead purposefully. Becoming a leader is a choice. It is the choice you have to make in your personal and professional life. Becoming a leader isn't easy and not everyone is willing to become the leader they need to be because they are unwilling or unable to move out of their comfort zones or they are happy in their mediocrity.

Being an Unstoppable Leader is about having the energy, passion, integrity, trustworthiness, accessibility, and character authenticity to be the very best leader you can be. Unstoppable Leadership is a conscious decision to take ownership for becoming and being a leader.

Unstoppable Leadership is about sharing a sense of purpose, an inspired vision, a believable mission, and a plan of action to the team. Unstoppable Leaders lead by example with a Frontline Approach.

Being an Unstoppable Leader requires you to be an inspiring role model and to inspire people. Unstoppable Leaders inspire people to work together and reach for goals that stretch them. Unstoppable Leaders instill trust, confidence, and commitment as they lead. Unstoppable Leaders inspire people to do great things.

LIFE AND LEADERSHIP

In my book, *You are Unstoppable*, I said that life is a journey. So is leadership. This book is about you and your journey to be the best person and leader that you can be. It will help you discover and identify who you are as a leader. Each day you have a choice to live an unstoppable and inspired life through your ability to lead yourself.

The foundation of your success begins with personal leadership and your personal commitment to be accountable and responsible for your life. Your leadership territory and terrain at times will be familiar, certain, and easy to chart your leadership path. Other times, the territory and terrain will be uncharted, uncertain, and difficult to chart. No matter the reason, you are here with the book in hand ready to unlock your Unstoppable Leadership.

Enjoy the journey of discovering your First Principles!

Chapter One

THE OWNERSHIP PRINCIPLE

Taking Responsibility of Your Leadership!

"Destiny is not a matter of chance; it is a matter of choice."
William Jennings Bryan

In 1983, I made a decision to join the United States Air Force. It was a life changing decision. In August, I arrived at Lackland Air Force Base in San Antonio, Texas, to start my introduction to the Air Force in Basic Military Training (BMT). It was the start of an inspiring journey that would last 28 years and take me to 32 different countries and all 50 States.

Upon arrival to BMT I realized a few things right away. First, Texas is hot, muggy, and you break a sweat just by breathing air. Second, I had no control of my life for the next six weeks. I was now the official property of the United States Air Force.

BMT provided me crystal clear clarity on the importance of taking ownership of my life and leadership. It taught me the value of self-respect, self-reliance, and self-efficacy.

It taught me the value of being intentionally focused on goals and achievement. It taught me that whatever you want or need in life takes time, intentional action, and persistent hard work to achieve. These indispensable lessons about life, leadership, and ownership changed my life and focus.

SELF-LEADERSHIP

If you want to succeed in BMT you need self-leadership. Upon arrival to Lackland Air Force Base you learn the meaning and importance of discipline. You learn how to fold your clothes, how to march, how to report to your leaders, and how to make your bed in accordance with the standards. This structured discipline approach became second nature and turned into self-discipline.

The key lesson that the disciplined approach of BMT taught me was that to be successful in life, and as a leader, you need self-leadership, self-control, and self-motivation. You need to own your life and leadership. You need self-discipline to train and develop yourself to prepare for the uncertainty of life's challenges.

Furthermore, you need to be a motivated self-starter who is a able to create and maintain your own drive. To succeed as an Unstoppable Leader you need a focused and disciplined approach to living your life, growing your leadership, and achieving your goals.

HARD WORK

BMT teaches you that hard work is a part of day-to-day life. So get used to it. Nothing is free or easy in the military. If it is important to you and you want to achieve it, you need to have the self-discipline and self-efficacy to work hard for it.

Hard work is the price you pay to achieve great things in your life. Let me reemphasize this point. Hard work is the price you pay to achieve great things in life. There are no free rides, everything has a cost. Free rides achieve mediocrity, complacency, and reduces your hunger for greatness.

Bottom Line: You must have the strength of character and the willingness to pay the price to become an Unstoppable Leader.

PLANNING/PREPARATION

During BMT, each day is planned and organized to maximize your day. There is no wasted time in BMT. Each day builds on the next and moves you closer to the goal of graduating and moving on to your technical school. This disciplined approach prepares you for a career in the military.

Just like in BMT, if you want to move ahead in life you must learn how to plan and prepare to maximize your time to achieve your life and leadership goals. Time is short so use it wisely. When you plan and prepare you are living your life by design and not by mere chance. You are preparing yourself to meet uncertainty head on.

DECISIONS

My Training Instructor (TI) informed me on the third day of BMT that, **"You will make or break your military career on the quality of your decisions. Everything you do from this day forward is a result of the decisions you make."** His words still ring true today. All life is a decision; consequentially, all leadership is a decision.

No matter what you do, you make choices and decisions daily. Your decisions may be small and inconsequential, like, what will I wear today? Or they can be life-impacting, like, should I join the military or go to college? One thing is for certain, not all decisions and choices will work the way you planned, while some will work exactly as you planned.

Nevertheless, you own the decision, its outcome, and its consequence. So, take the time to think about the outcome and the second, third, and fourth order of effects on your life before you make the decision.

You are responsible and accountable for your life, leadership, and its eventual outcome. No one else is responsible or accountable for how your life turns out. No one else is responsible for your leadership decisions or actions. Your life and leadership are the product of how well you plan and prepare.

Each day you are empowered to make a choice and take a chance to create your destiny. Without knowing where you want to go and then making the right choice, you will live your life by chance.

In every leading situation you face, you can choose how to respond and what to do or not do. Victor Frankl and Stephen Covey both explain that you have a choice in every situation. The choice is between stimulus and response. The space between stimulus and response is your greatest freedom; it is your choice to be proactive or reactive.

You are in control of your response. You choose your destiny through your deliberate choices and actions. Your destiny is the sum total of all your life choices and actions toward achieving your lifelong dreams and goals. Your life is a series of daily choices and actions. From the moment you wake up until the moment you fall asleep at night, you are creating your destiny.

Your daily choices are the beginning point of your destiny. Some of your daily choices may influence your life greatly, but all your choices have an impact on your life.

Understanding how you make choices is important because your choices are a reflection of your values, beliefs, and worldview. Each choice moves you further down your journey in life. Your choices and actions determine your destiny. Your destiny is your untapped potential waiting to be unleashed.

It is your choice to make your destiny successful. Your true success in leadership is determined by the disciplined, purposeful, and measured choices you make each day to achieve your goals and reach your objectives.

The more your goals represent your values, beliefs, and worldview, the more likely you are to achieve them. Through your vision and foresight you know what your leadership strategy should be and how you plan to achieve it. However, achieving your goals is best not left up to chance, but from well thought out choices.

A disciplined approach to making choices does not mean you stop taking risks or chances in life. It just means you understand the consequences of the decision before you make it.

Ben Franklin's quote about chess is a good example of a disciplined approach to decision-making.

> Chess teaches foresight, by having to plan ahead; vigilance, by having to keep watch over the whole chess board; caution, by having to restrain ourselves from making hasty moves; and finally, we learn from chess the greatest maxim in life - that even when everything seems to be going badly for us we should not lose heart, but always hoping for a change for the better, steadfastly continue searching for the solutions to our problems.

THE FIRST PRINCIPLES

Your choices can create chances or opportunities for you to make an impact in your life, your family, your community, or your organization. By taking the risk or a calculated chance, you can change your life and increase your leadership ability.

- Taking a chance as a leader may offer you an opportunity to grow exponentially, open a door that was first unseen, or see the new stepping-stones paving the path to your goals

- Taking a chance is being willing to step outside your comfort zone to pursue your passion and purpose

- Taking a chance can mean the difference between a mediocre or a marvelous life

One thing for sure, no matter if it is in life or leading people, change is a constant. Change can be good or it can be bad, but change is inevitable in life. As you make choices and take chances, you change. You grow, you develop, and you reinvent yourself as you grow and develop as a leader.

In addition, as you change over the years you are not the same person you were as you began your journey. Nor should you be the same. Life would be stagnant and unproductive if you did not grow and change. You are the only one that can make the choice and take the chance to develop yourself and make your lifelong dreams become a reality.

Ultimately, you reap what you sow and your destiny is a direct reflection on the choices that you make toward achieving the goals that you set for your success. In everything you do, set your leadership on the foundation of your character, competence, courage, commitment, communication, connections, and choices to move forward.

Take the time and the risk to conquer your fears. Take the risk to lead in the great adventure called leadership. It is your leadership; take the risk and become an Unstoppable Leader.

ACTIONS

Each order given during BMT required some type of action to carry out the order. First, there is a preparatory command that indicates a preparation phase before the command of execution.

A good example of this two phased command is "Forward, March." When the TI yelled "Forward, March," you put your feet and brain into action to carry out the command. The preparatory command indicated a direction and the command of execution indicated the action. Each step is required to achieve the desired results.

Your decisions are just like the preparatory command "Forward." It is not until you apply direct and intentional actions do they go from concept to reality.

A decision to do something without an action applied is just a passing thought and is useless. Your actions to complete your decisions will determine what you can and will achieve. You must take action in life to achieve success. **Bottom Line: You must be a leader of action to achieve great success.**

RESPONSIBILITY/ACCOUNTABILITY

Along with my TI's information on decisions, he constantly drilled into us that we are responsible and accountable for our actions in the Air Force. He did not want to hear our excuses or hear us pass the blame on circumstances or on another person. **"You are responsible and accountable for how your Air Force career turns out. NO ONE ELSE."**

PERSISTENCE/PERSEVERANCE

The best BMT lesson I learned was to never give up on yourself or your goals. BMT is intended to break you down then build you up so you are ready for the challenges of the military.

BMT teaches you to persevere and persist to reach for your goals. It teaches you to keep intentionally pressing toward your goals until you achieve them-- never give up on yourself and your dreams and each day keep pressing on toward the finish line!

I will be the first to tell you that the military life is not easy nor is it for everyone. It takes time to learn how to adapt and adopt your life to military standards.

However, you learn very quickly what you are made of and what you are capable of doing.

It teaches you to persist and persevere if you want to have a successful career. Each day you lead is a challenge. You will need to persevere and persist to meet the leadership challenges of leading people, managing organizational assets, and achieving team and organizational goals. Leadership, at times, requires a strong will and dogged perseverance to achieve results.

These lessons continue to be invaluable to me throughout my career and in life. These valuable life and leadership lessons helped me shape and mold my Air Force Career and my leadership.

The clarity and focus these lessons provided gave me the passion to achieve my goals. Life is what you make of it and it begins with taking 100% control of your life and leadership.

OWN IT!

It is your leadership…**Own it!** It is up to you…you are the key to your leadership and becoming an Unstoppable Leader. The true key, if you want to be an Unstoppable Leader, is to take 100% control of your leadership.

If you want to succeed as a leader, then you need to create the leadership outcomes you desire. You are the owner of your successes, failures, emotions, and feelings. Being an Unstoppable Leader is a realization that leadership begins with self-leadership. To be an Unstoppable Leader you need to take ownership of your life and understand who you are and how you operate as a human being first before you can lead others.

Self-leadership requires a deliberate and disciplined approach. It is a mindset concerning actions, behaviors, and performance. It is a conscious choice of self-regulation, self-control, and self-efficacy. Taking ownership, responsibility, and accountability makes you a stronger leader.

An Unstoppable Leader needs self-insight into how they operate, how they make decisions, and how to treat people, in order to lead people. Being an Unstoppable Leader requires that your life and your leadership are wholly integrated. You must fully understand who you are, what you can do, and what you can offer before you can lead others effectively and efficiently.

You must live with integrity of character, honed competence, undeniable courage, and fully committed to living congruent with your values, beliefs, and worldview in order to lead.

Unfortunately, too many leaders refuse to discover who they are before they begin to lead, then fail miserably. When you begin to comprehend your capabilities, abilities, desires, and dreams, you begin to understand your life and leadership.

Becoming an Unstoppable Leader requires a focused process of self-leadership. Before you can lead others you have to recognize your true self. Becoming an Unstoppable Leader means you begin to shape your vision, mission, objectives, and goals for your future and then follow through with deliberate actions.

OWN IT WITH PRIDE

You must take ownership for your life and leadership. Ownership, Responsibility, and Accountability means you own your choices, actions, results, and outcomes. Accountability and responsibility are must haves for an Unstoppable Leader to possess. Unstoppable Leaders take responsibility to be a part of the solution and not the problem.

Leaders with a high internal locus of control are in control of their life and leadership. They seek to shape their outcomes by putting the necessary effects into their lives. They see accountability and responsibility as the way to control their actions and consequences.

An Unstoppable Leader takes responsibility for the outcomes in their professional life. Taking ownership of your life and leadership is telling everyone that you are accountable and responsible.

It is your John Hancock moment. If you take the time to look at the Declaration of Independence you will gravitate to John Hancock's signature. It is very prominent at the bottom center of the document. With flourish and pride he signed his name to the document.

He was not ashamed of signing the document and he believed in the document's cause. John Hancock wanted King George to see his signature on the document from his throne in England. You need to do the same with your life and leadership. Own it so everyone knows it was you. **Own it with PRIDE!**

TOP DOWN RESPONSIBILITY

Effective leadership begins at the top and permeates throughout the organization at all levels. This is a crucial factor in assuring that leadership is an organization-wide capability.

Unstoppable Leaders must be worthy of their people's trust and confidence. The impact of successful leadership cascades across all departments in an organization and can affect the morale of each person. Leaders are the linchpin to the organization's culture and organizational effectiveness.

Leaders at every level in an organization must accept the responsibility to lead, take ownership of their part of the mission, and develop their people. A culture of accountability and responsibility is established through solid standards of performance and leadership for people to live by.

Standards and expectations draw a clear line between what is acceptable and unacceptable performance. Standards and expectations give clarity of accountability and responsibility. Credibility and trustworthiness are the foundations of leadership.

Trust grows when expectations are clear, when people know what they have been empowered to do, and when they can focus on doing it. People trust a leader who understands the overall mission and vision of the organization, who inspires them, and provides a sense of higher purpose.

HOLD YOURSELF ACCOUNTABLE

Responsibility and accountability are cornerstones of Unstoppable Leadership. Before you can hold others accountable, you first must hold yourself accountable. Accountability means you are willing to bear the yoke of leadership and be responsible for your actions, choices, and decisions.

You cannot lead effectively without responsibility and accountability. Taking responsibility and accountability for your actions and those of your people means taking ownership for the results, outcomes, and consequences.

Unstoppable Leadership is about you earning and maintaining your personal credibility and trustworthiness. You are accountable for your choices in life, how well you prepare yourself in life, how you persevere and persist against the odds, and moreover, you are accountable for your outlook and attitude about your life.

You must take accountability for your life or someone else will. No one else is responsible or accountable for how your professional life turns out.

The outcome of your personal and professional life is the product of your decisions, how well you planned your life, and your intentional actions. **Bottom Line: An Unstoppable Leader needs to be responsible and accountable for their personal and professional life.**

HOLD YOUR TEAM ACCOUNTABLE

Leadership is complex, challenging, and dynamic. It is not for those weak in character or integrity. Leadership will beat you down if you are not prepared for its challenges.

But leadership can allow you to soar on wings like an eagle if you rise to meet each challenge and overcome them. It can be exhilarating, frustrating, full of accomplishment, and at times leave you empty.

Leadership is leading people each day to meet the organizational mission while at the same time helping them to achieve their goals and desires. As an Unstoppable Leader you are responsible for your actions, the results of your team, and the productivity of your organization.

In your professional life and in your private life, if people do not believe in you, they will not trust you. Being responsible for the results and outcomes of your team is leadership business. To ensure the desired outcome and results for your team you need to establish clear standards for performance and reward those who achieve excellence.

A willingness to accept responsibility is a critical part of being an Unstoppable Leader. Set high standards and hold yourself and your team responsible and accountable for their performance. You must take full responsibility for your leadership.

As a leader, when you take responsibility you set the example for others to follow. Your team will recognize and understand the importance of accepting responsibility by a leader's action.

100 PERCENT OWNERSHIP

Taking 100% ownership starts with a deep belief in yourself and the confidence that you have in yourself to succeed. Confidence is vital in leadership because it is the key ingredient in making a difference and will impact how you lead each day.

Confidence is your inner motivator and driver of becoming and being a leader. Responsibility is taking ownership for the task or job at hand and ensuring it is accomplished. As stated earlier, accountability is taking ownership for your actions, decisions, consequences, and results to accomplish the task or job.

THE IMPORTANCE OF DECISIONS

You make choices in your life each day. You can choose to be intentional and proactive and take control of your decisions or you can react to them like a victim of circumstance.

- Each decision is an opportunity to make an impact
- Each decision is made from your intentional action, the impact of the action, and the results of that action

You are responsible and accountable for your leadership decisions. Each day you need to intentionally identify and evaluate information and then use the information to make a decision, take action, and critically analyze the outcome to understand the second, third, and fourth order of effects of the decision.

DECISIONS AND CHOICES

You need to own your decisions, choices, and mistakes and be ready and willing to take the essential steps to learn from them. You need to believe in your ability to affect your life's outcomes in order to have the confidence and courage to meet the challenges of leadership.

Decision-making is a required and necessary leadership skill in a complex and chaotic world. Decision-making is a risk, but a risk worth taking. A leader who will not make a decision because of fear of failure or fear of the consequences is worthless to their team and their organization.

It is vital, no imperative, that a leader be able to make educated and workable decisions amid uncertainty and ambiguity. Your team and your organization is depending on you to make decisions. Your leadership decisions are the single most important factor that drives your unstoppable leadership.

Leadership focus, clarity, and intentionality gives you an opportunity to effectively look at how you will make a decision by evaluating the second, third, and fourth order of effects of your choices.

This clarity and focus will help you to select leadership actions that create the desired outcomes you want as a leader. In the end, you are ultimately accountable and responsible for your leadership decisions and actions.

Leadership decision-making requires that a leader has the ability to take facts, data, and disparate information, and integrate them together into actionable knowledge. A leader then uses the integrated and actionable knowledge to make educated decisions that are achievable to the team and organizational goals.

To be an effective decision-maker you must be proactive and stay abreast of issues, threats, trends, and opportunities to reduce uncertainty and ambiguity. When you take the time to become fully aware of new leadership opportunities, you can then create new possibilities for yourself, your team, and organization.

As a leader of a team or in an organization you need to take the time to assimilate data and facts into actionable data. When you make leadership decisions you will reduce ambiguity and uncertainty and provide clarity and continued focus for you and your team. By choosing to lead with focus, you begin to see the simple answer to complex issues. By choosing to lead with focus and intentionality, your leadership has leadership clarity.

SUCCESSES AND FAILURES

Taking ownership of success is easy because success makes you feel good about yourself and your abilities. Success gives you a boost in your confidence level and your leadership ability.

Failure on the other hand can decrease your confidence level and cause you to question your ability as a leader to get the job done. Failure has a way of making you retreat and lick your wounds versus look for a new way to achieve success.

However, both success and failure shape your leadership. Success lets you know when you are doing it right and are making good decisions. Failure tells you that you need to review and reflect on your decisions and actions. It also lets you know that you need to improve. **Bottom Line: You are accountable and responsible for both the successes and failures as a leader.**

THE FORGE DISCOVERY PROCESS

The FORGE Discovery Process is a focused and disciplined approach to developing your Unstoppable Leadership. Unstoppable Leadership requires you to discover and become more aware of yourself as a leader. Becoming an Unstoppable Leader requires hard work, integrity, intentionality, self-discipline, sacrifice, commitment, courage, character, and competence.

Integrity, character, and competence are the indispensable elements of Unstoppable Leadership. Becoming an Unstoppable Leader requires growth, development, and reinventing oneself, not once, but over and over again. Unstoppable Leadership involves being responsible and accountable for all that happens or fails to happen.

- The FORGE Discovery Process is about being proactive, taking charge, and leading your life and leadership; a leader must understand why they want to be a leader

- The FORGE Discovery Process allows you to discover and become more aware of yourself as a leader; it is about making the choices each day to determine your destiny and future life

- The FORGE Discovery Process guides you to start looking at the *Why* of your leadership and helps you define your purpose, your vision, and your goals

The FORGE Discovery process begins with five defining questions you need to answer before you can start authoring your Unstoppable Leadership. By reviewing, reflecting, and doing a deep dive on your motives and intentions you start discovering your

Unstoppable Leadership. Under each main question are several leading questions to help you further define your leadership.

- **WHY DO YOU WANT TO BE AN UNSTOPPABLE LEADER?**

  - Why is it important for you to lead and influence people?

  - What impact do you want to have?

  - Do you have a passion for people?

- **WHO ARE YOU?**

  - Do you understand your life through Personal Insight and Personal Mastery?

  - Do you understand how your purpose, values, beliefs, worldview, and experiences, influences your leadership and your decisions?

  - Do you understand that who you are as a person is who you are as a leader?

- **WHAT KIND OF LEADER DO YOU WANT TO BECOME?**

  - What does your leadership look like?

  - Will you inspire and encourage?

- What difference will you make?
- Do you have the ability to be flexible and adaptive?

- **WHERE DO YOU SEE YOURSELF AS A LEADER?**
  - What kind of job, lifestyle, and achievements do you want?
  - What is your vision and mission for your leadership and your team?
  - Do you know where you will be, as a leader, in 5, 10, or 20 years?

- **WHEN AND HOW DO YOU PLAN TO ACHIEVE YOUR LEADERSHIP END STATE?**
  - What is your action plan to achieve your Unstoppable Life and Leadership?
  - What is your timeline and milestones for achieving your Unstoppable Leadership?

The FORGE Discovery Process helps you to define and refine who you are as a leader and what value and impact you will have. **Bottom Line: Your Unstoppable Leadership is a direct result of the decisions you make, the actions you take, and experience you get from your challenges and trials.**

THE FORGE DEVELOPMENT PROCESS

In my book, *You are Unstoppable: Unleash Your Inspired Life,* I talk about the FORGE Development Process for developing your life. The FORGE Development Process is a detailed and proactive way of thinking about your life and its direction.

The FORGE Development Process comes from the fact that as a leader you are constantly going through trials, tribulations, and challenges as you grow and go through life. Your life and your leadership are forged by those trials and tribulations.

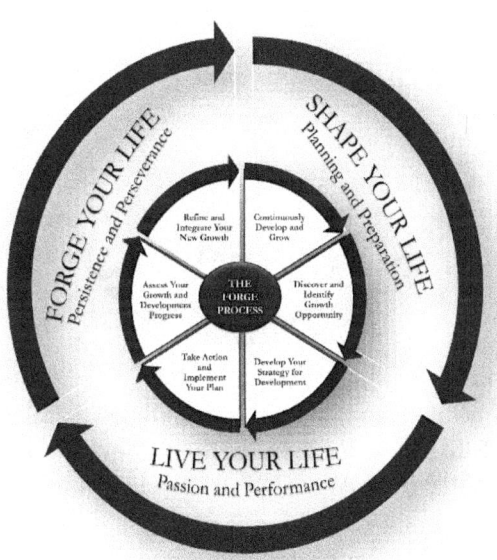

The FORGE Development Process details the effects that you need to put in your life to change or direct the outcomes. It is a way of thinking about the second, third, and fourth order of effects that can happen and asking the "what ifs" of your life and preparing yourself for the future.

The FORGE Development Process model has three distinct areas of growth and development.

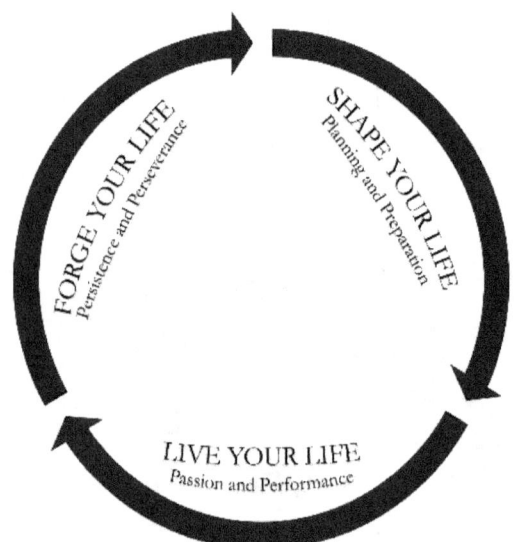

- The outside area contains the three phases of the FORGE Development Process. The first phase is **SHAPE YOUR LIFE** and is the planning and preparation phase of your life. This phase is about knowing who you are, what you are capable of doing, and what actions do you need to take to shape your Unstoppable Life.

- The second phase is **LIVE YOUR LIFE** and is the passion and performance phase of your life. This phase is about the passion, enthusiasm, and energy you have in life and how well you are living your Unstoppable Life. This is the execution phase of your life plan and you begin to move from the "as-is" to the "to-be" you.

- The third phase is **FORGE YOUR LIFE** and is the persistence and perseverance phase of your life. This phase is about reevaluating your growth and development strategy, incorporating new growth into your life and leadership, and pressing forward in living your Unstoppable Life.

As you persevere, persist, and finally conquer your hardships, you are made stronger and more committed to becoming an Unstoppable Leader.

The true key to being an Unstoppable Leader is in what you learn from and how you respond to the hardship and adversity. Remember: it isn't your problems that define you, but how you react and respond to them.

Do not fall into the trap of following the path of least resistance. It may work for water, but it does not work in real life. How you choose to shape yourself as you go through the crucibles of life and leadership will make you an Unstoppable Leader.

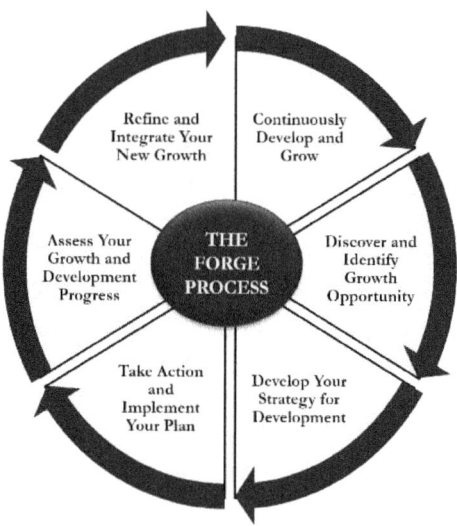

The next part of the FORGE Development Process is the inner circle of the model. The circle contains the six elements of developing your life's strategy and life plan. The six elements are:

- **Continuously Develop and Grow:** This stage is where you begin to evaluate yourself again to find out what other skills, talents, or mindsets you need to acquire after you have grown in an area. By using the FORGE Development Process you can grow and develop yourself and become a better leader.

- **Discover and Identify Growth Opportunity:** The Discover and Identify Growth Opportunity stage requires self-awareness and self-understanding. Do you know all your talents, gifts, opportunities, and capabilities? Do you know what growth opportunities you need to develop you for future challenges?

- **Develop Your Strategy for Development:** Once you can answer the questions above, you can move on to the Develop Your Strategy for Development. This stage is where you develop your life change strategy to grow in those areas of opportunity you have discovered and identified. Your strategy must focus on the desired effects, future states, or outcomes you want to develop or change in the next year.

- **Take Action and Implement Your Plan:** This stage is where the actual execution of the growth and development strategies take place in order for change to happen.

- **Assess Your Growth and Development Progress:** The assessment stage focuses on the impact of the change by assessing the results of the effects on your daily life. This is your map and compass stage. This stage is also where you assess your plan's effectiveness against the inchstones, milestones, and timelines you have laid in the plan.

- **Refine and Integrate Your New Growth:** This stage is where your change strategies are implemented to produce new levels of knowledge of self-awareness. Your outcome has been achieved and you have acquired a new skill, talent, or mindset to help you continue to grow and develop in your growth areas.

To be unstoppable you need to choose your responses and outcomes. **Remember: being a leader means you will face challenges and setbacks, and you must learn, adapt, and overcome them and turn them into your successes.**

SUMMARY

It is your leadership…**OWN It!** You own your decisions, choices, and you are accountable and responsible for the actions of your team. Each day you make decisions that will make an impact, will change the course of your team, and will move you from your comfort zones. **Commit yourself to taking 100% ownership of your leadership.**

THE FIRST PRINCIPLES

CHARACTER CHECK

1. Do you own your Life and Leadership?

2. Are You willing to take the risk to be an Unstoppable Leader?

3. Are you willing to be responsible and accountable for your decisions and actions?

LOOKING INTO THE MIRROR

After reading this chapter, review and reflect on the ideas and concepts presented. Think about what opportunities, challenges, resources, or blind spots you may encounter when you begin your growth and development journey.

Use the following questions to help you grow and develop.

1. How will I incorporate this principle into my leadership development?

2. What opportunity and resources exist for me to use this principle this week, this year?

3. What blind spots may derail me from using this principle?

COMMITMENT TIME

- ✓ It is your leadership…OWN It!
- ✓ You own your decisions and choices
- ✓ You are accountable and responsible for the actions of your team
- ✓ You are the owner of your successes, failures, emotions, and feelings
- ✓ Each day you make decisions that will make an impact, change the course of your team, and move you from your comfort zones
- ✓ Commit yourself to taking 100% ownership of your leadership
- ✓ Before you can hold others accountable, you first must hold yourself accountable
- ✓ Credibility and trustworthiness are key foundations of leadership
- ✓ Being responsible for the results and outcomes of your team is leadership business
- ✓ In everything you do, set your leadership on the foundation of your character, competence, courage, commitment, and choices to move forward

LEADERSHIP NOTES

CHAPTER TWO

THE AWARENESS PRINCIPLE

BEING AN AWAKE AND ALIVE LEADER!

Absurdum est ut alios regat, qui seipsum regere nescit
(It is absurd that a man should rule others, who cannot rule himself)
Latin Proverb

In 2004, I assumed the Command Chief position at Altus Air Force Base. The Command Chief is a senior leader position and is responsible for advising the commander and staff on mission effectiveness, professional development, military readiness, training, utilization, health, morale, and welfare of the command's enlisted.

The Command Chief is to serve as a role model, lead by example, and to serve the commander and the enlisted force. A key role for this leader is to prepare and develop Airmen for their future leadership opportunities and roles. To fulfill this role I communicated quite frequently with all Airmen in the Wing and I took every opportunity to communicate to the emerging leaders at the Altus Air Force Base Airman's Leadership School. (ALS).

The ALS is the first level of professional military education and deliberate leadership development for emerging enlisted Airmen. It is a deliberate and disciplined development program focused on preparing effective front-line leaders/supervisors. The key focus learning areas of ALS are developing leadership skills and abilities, understanding effective communication and its role in leading others, and understanding your chosen career--the profession of arms.

The Airmen that attend ALS are the future leaders of the Air Force. My leadership message below focused on becoming and being a leader in the Air Force, the expectations of being a leader, and their role in their own development of their competence and character.

> As a leader you have an opportunity to make an impact on your organization and your people every day, so the first step in being a great leader is to know yourself. The journey to becoming and being a leader starts with the journey to truly understand who you are, what you are capable of accomplishing, and why you want to lead.
>
> Becoming a leader requires that you take the time early in your career to grow and develop your

understanding of your core values, core beliefs, and your worldview. Understanding how you make choices is a critical component of your leadership. Your values and your beliefs motivate and drive you and can affect your leadership effectiveness.

This is the first and most important step for a leader because these three define who you are and will affect how you make life and leadership decisions. Self-awareness is hard work and requires a lifelong commitment to self-discovery and to persistence, perseverance, and patience to build upon the foundation of who you are, and to lay the groundwork for your leadership.

The best investment you can ever make in your life and your leadership is to invest in yourself, your talents, and your skills--your competence; and to understand your values, beliefs, and worldview--your character.

General Norman Schwarzkopf, when he addressed the Cadet Corps at West Point stated that: *"To be a 21st-century leader, you must have two things: competence and character...To lead in the 21st Century, to take soldiers, sailors, airmen, marines, coastguardsmen into battle, you will be required to have both competence and character."*

Character and competence are the lifeblood of your leadership. They are the double-edged sword of your leadership. On one side is your competence--your skills, talents, abilities, and capabilities. On the other side is your character--your values, beliefs, and worldview.

In addition, running down the center of the sword is your integrity. Integrity is the key ingredient that fuses your competence and character together. Resting at the very tip of the sword, at the point where your competence and character merge, is your leadership credibility.

You must hone both sides of the sword to be a great leader. Your competence and character must be razor sharp to lead in the 21st Century and the uncertainty and chaos of today's world.

Just like I expressed to the emerging leaders of the Air Force, becoming an Unstoppable Leader begins with you. It begins with a condition of your heart and starts with desire and passion to make a difference. Being an Unstoppable Leader is about having the energy, passion, integrity, trustworthiness, accessibility, and character authenticity to be the very best leader you can be.

Unstoppable Leadership is an inside-out process and is shaped by your values, character, choices, opportunities, experiences, and your worldview.

Unstoppable Leadership is not about you, it is about the people you influence and inspire. Unstoppable Leadership is about creating a positive culture to bring out the creativity and innovation of your team. Unstoppable Leadership is a powerful belief that you can make a difference and have an impact.

SELF-AWARENESS

Ipsa Scientia Potestas Est
(Knowledge is power)
Sir Francis Bacon

The first real mark of becoming an Unstoppable Leader is Self-Awareness. Leadership begins from within, and who you are as a leader comes from who you are at your inner core.

Self-awareness means you understand your inner core. Before you can lead others, you have to recognize your true self. Unfortunately, too many leaders refuse to discover who they truly are before they begin to lead and then struggle when adversity comes their way.

Becoming an Unstoppable Leader requires that you are well grounded in your character and that your core values, beliefs, and worldview are integrated into your leadership.

Self-awareness means you have clarity of your passions, strengths, weaknesses, opportunities, and threats. Without personal clarity it is impossible to have professional clarity and therefore impossible to lead congruently with your inner core.

You need to have a deep understanding of who you really are before you lead. You need to know and understand your strengths, weaknesses, capabilities, abilities, and your emotions. Nothing is more important to your success of becoming an Unstoppable Leader than your self-awareness.

Self-awareness is believing in yourself with conviction and commitment. It is an awareness of your strengths and your challenges. Nosce Te Ipsum is Latin for Know Thyself. The saying is attributed to many Greek and Roman philosophers to include Socrates, Aristotle, Heraclitus, and Cicero.

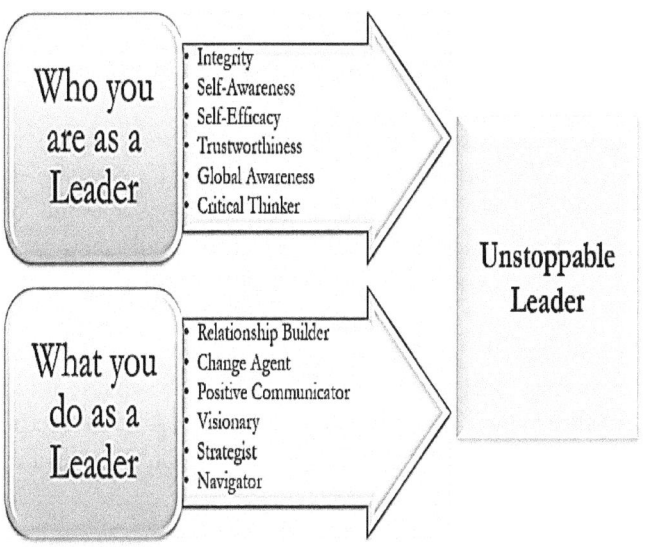

Self-awareness gives a leader a greater understanding of his or her values, beliefs, and worldview. It provides insight on the how and why they make decisions. Self-awareness is about understanding your self-efficacy, self-leadership, and intentional clarity.

Knowing yourself improves your self-discipline and self-control in different situations, allowing you to work with others during challenging and demanding problems more skillfully and diplomatically. It allows you to use the right capabilities at the right time and in the right situational context.

Finally, knowing yourself likewise provides you more confidence in developing yourself for the present operations and future challenges.

YOUR MEASURING TOOLS

When we bought our first house we decided to build a 1200 foot addition to the house. This was a big project and several measuring tools were needed to ensure the footings, walls, and roof were built accurately and the plumbing installed correctly.

I needed to ensure the addition was built in accordance with building codes, but also to ensure it did not fall down. The measuring tools needed were a tape measure, a carpenter's level, a square, a plumb line, and a 360-degree laser level.

Each tool had a specific purpose for building the addition. The tape measure ensured the accuracy of the length of each footing, each board, and each wall.

The carpenter's level ensured that the foundation and walls were level and true. The square measured and ensured that corners were at 90 degrees to each other and squared. The plumb line ensured that the constructed walls were upright, straight, and vertical to the square.

The laser level established a straight and true line 360 degrees around the room to ensure construction elements were aligned along a lined path.

These tools were important to ensuring that each construction phase and each element was measured accurately, square, level, and plumb in order to ensure the fundamental structural integrity of the addition. Each tool ensured that a standard was adhered to and measured to ensure accuracy.

Just like building a house and ensuring that it is set to a standard to ensure its overall integrity and authenticity, your character needs to be built to ensure its integrity and authenticity are set on a solid foundation. Your measuring tools are not the tape measure, levels, square, or plumb line, but your purpose, values, beliefs, and worldview.

LEADERSHIP DRIVERS

This theme of understanding yourself is also a key principle many of today's leadership authors point to as the beginning point for all leaders.

If you desire to lead and influence others, then you need to be cognizant of your actions, principles, and beliefs and be aware of how they shape you and influence others.

Your inner core influences how you operate in the world. Your values, beliefs, and worldview influence your priorities, decisions, actions, and your behavior. Through the influence of your inner core you prioritize your results. Part of self-discovery is defining your core values, your beliefs, and worldview.

Along with your life's purpose, your values, beliefs, and worldview are the lenses that you see the world through, handle challenges with, and approach your leadership decisions by. The choices you make in life define who you are as a leader.

PURPOSE

The first thing you need to do is to awaken the leader within you. It is about discovering your true purpose. It is about seizing control of your life by discovering your purpose. To be an effective and successful person you need to figure out what is important to you, what matters in your life, and what you stand for.

You need to live out your purpose authentically and daily. You need to passionately pursue your purpose in life and relentlessly challenge yourself to become better each day.

Purpose is the "why" you do what you do and self-awareness is how you discover your purpose. Finding and fulfilling your leadership purpose is your key to success as a leader.

How do you discover your purpose? Your purpose is a matter of reflecting on who you are, what excites and motivates you, and what you feel called to do. Your purpose is the true essence of who you are as a person and a leader.

Your purpose drives you, influences you, and shapes your actions and reactions to life. Just as you need oxygen to breathe and survive, you need purpose to thrive and survive. Discovering your purpose is a process of self-discovery and self-awareness and to be effective, you need to be serving your purpose.

Living with purpose means your life and leadership are congruent. Purpose expresses most deeply what makes you a unique individual.

- Your purpose defines who you are, how you live your life, and how you lead

- Your purpose motivates and drives you throughout life; your purpose influences your whole life

- Your purpose is the compass that helps you chart your way in the world and in life

- Your life and your leadership are driven by one thing...your purpose in life

VALUES, BELIEFS, AND WORLDVIEW

Values are those core principles that you hold dear, live your life around, and are unchanging. Your core values are shaped by your core belief system. Values are those things that you hold most dear in your life; family, faith, freedom, human dignity, respect for others, and integrity are just a few examples.

These values and beliefs shape your character and shape how you look at the world. Personal values are aspects of life you think are important to live your life with, such as integrity, excellence, or service.

- Your values drive your behavior and shape your leadership behaviors, actions, and decisions

- Your values are your way of making sense of what is going on in the world and how you choose to act and react as a leader

As a leader, you need to understand that you are a complex network of values, beliefs, ideas, traits, capabilities, talents, and life experiences. This complex network is your character and leadership DNA. Your leadership is the outward expression of your purpose, values, beliefs, and worldview.

Your character is your inner workings of beliefs, motives, values, desires, behaviors, and principles that drive and shape your actions as a leader. Knowing your true self makes you more effective in your life. Discovering your true self is important if you want to be a leader.

When you are living congruent to your purpose, beliefs, and values, then you are living authentically. Values are those core beliefs that you hold dear, live your life around, and are unchanging. Your core beliefs define your worldview.

Your worldview is how you look at the world through your values, beliefs, and purpose. Leading with your purpose and your core values ensures your life and leadership are congruent.

EXPERIENCES

Your leadership and life experiences also act as leadership drivers. They shape, mold, and challenge you to rethink, reframe, and reinvent your leadership. Your success and failures are a key tool in your leadership DNA. It is through these leadership experiences that you begin to understand your leadership capabilities and faults.

Your learning experiences arise from day-to-day activities, from moving out of your comfort zone and through your trials and challenges. Do not run from your problems or challenges, face them head on and tackle them. It isn't your problems that define you as a leader, but how you react and act on them.

Remember, being a leader means you will face challenges and setbacks, but the true skill is to learn, adapt, and overcome them and turn them into your successes. It is through that forging process that your mettle is tested and you are forged into the leader you want to become.

A critical component of pressing forward is reviewing what your experiences have taught you. Your experiences are stepping-stones of progress. You will learn more from your mistakes, errors, and challenges than you will learn from your successes. Why? Because it means you are taking the risk to live your life to its fullest. Do not be afraid of failing from time to time. Every challenge will teach you valuable leadership lessons that will grow and forge you.

THE UNSTOPPABLE MODEL

The Unstoppable Model builds upon my original F(X) Leadership Development Model from the book, *F(X) Leadership Unleashed*, but solely focuses on personal development instead of organizational development.

The two main parts of the model are the inner core and the outer rings. The inner core consists of the Delta symbol, 5Cs and your values, beliefs, and worldview. The outer rings contain the discovery processes of your Personal Insight and Personal Mastery.

The Unstoppable Model focuses on a whole person concept and is a disciplined inside-outside approach to growth, development, and reinvention focused on all aspects of your life. The Unstoppable Model is a constant look at your life as you grow, develop, and learn more about who you are and what you are capable of throughout your life.

You must lead yourself and take ownership of your life. Personal leadership is a key part of living an Unstoppable Life and living abundantly.

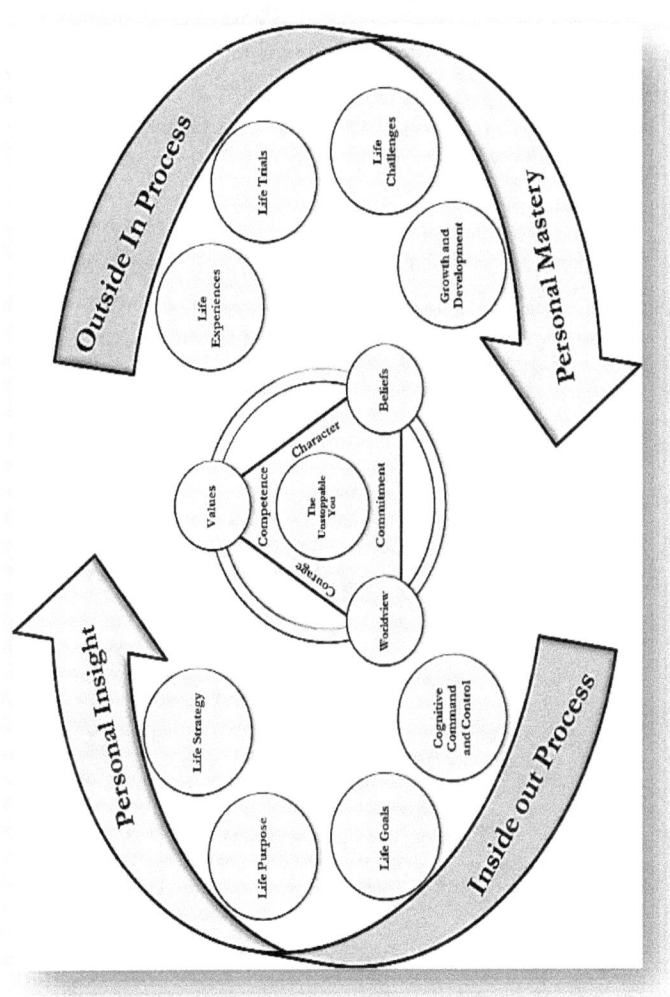

THE FIRST PRINCIPLES

THE INNER CORE

Each day you have a choice to live an Unstoppable and Inspired life through your ability to lead yourself. The foundation of your success begins with personal leadership and your personal commitment to be accountable and responsible for your life.

The first part of the Unstoppable Model is the 5Cs--Character, Competence, Courage, Commitment, Choices, and the Delta Symbol. This is the most explosive part of your life and is constantly changing and developing each day.

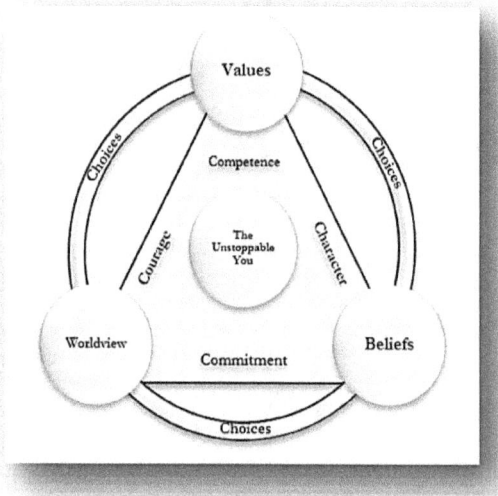

(**Note:** In Chapter 3, the Authenticity Principle, I expand on the 5Cs Inner Core Model to the 7Cs Leadership Model and include two critical leadership components--Communication and Connections.)

Your values, beliefs, and worldview are the next part of the model and are the constants in your life. Your core values drive your life choices and your decisions about when you want to lead, how you want to lead, and how much you want to lead. These two parts make up the inner core of the Unstoppable Model. Your character, competence, courage, commitment, values, beliefs, and worldview are key parts of being Unstoppable.

These provide you with the solid foundation you need to build upon each day to create an Unstoppable Life and to be an Unstoppable Leader.

By understanding your inner core you create greater life opportunities through your outer rings. The key to understanding your true self is to know who you are as a person first.

- What do you believe down deep inside your soul?

- What do you value in life?

- What motivates you to be the best person you can be?

Knowing your true self makes you more effective in your life. To understand your true self you need to understand what your beliefs are. A core belief is what your conviction is regarding God, people, concepts, or the world.

Your core beliefs are those indispensable elements to defining your life and living it authentically. Your core beliefs are the center or core of what you believe about life, death, religion, morals, what is good, what is bad, what is right, and what is wrong. Your core beliefs allow you to weather every storm, trial, and tribulation.

Without solid core beliefs, your personal way of life will be empty and you will be indecisive at every opportunity or challenge in life. The choices you make in life define who you are as a person.

Your core beliefs define your worldview. Your core beliefs define your core values and shape your life on a daily basis. Values are those core beliefs that you hold dear, live your life around, and are unchanging.

The Outer Rings

The outside rings of the Unstoppable Model represent two areas of personal growth and development--Personal Insight and Personal Mastery. As a life leader, you must learn to lead yourself effectively each day and stay focused on achieving your life goals.

Personal Insight

Personal Insight is an intentional process of discovering and understanding who you are, what you believe in, and your life purpose. Personal Insight embraces the concept of Nosce Te Ipsum (To Know Yourself). It is an inward look at your life through a deliberate process of reflection and self-study. Personal Insight helps you to know your values, beliefs, worldview, life purpose, and define your authentic character.

It is an honest self-assessment about your strengths and weaknesses. Your core values are shaped by your core belief system. Values are those things that you hold most dear in your life: family, faith, freedom, human dignity, respect for others, and integrity are just a few examples. These values and beliefs shape your character and shape how you see the world.

Personal Insight provides you with the personal confidence you need to plan and prepare for the future through an increased self-awareness of what you want to achieve in life. This self-awareness provides you increased and strategic clarity to develop an inspiring life vision.

Using self-insight, you can determine the approach you need to take to become more effective and proactive in your life. It allows you to meet the challenges of life head on without fear or uncertainty.

Truly understanding who you are and how you operate as a person can better help you understand how to grow, develop, and reinvent yourself for life.

Through Personal Insight you establish an inspiring vision for your life, define a Mission Statement, Life Goals, and a Life Strategy to achieve an Unstoppable Life.

Personal Mastery

Personal Mastery is a commitment to self-discipline, continuous growth, and development. It is a disciplined approach to honing your personal competence by developing your eight personal development areas--personal, professional, leadership, spiritual, emotional, physical, mental, and social disciplines.

Personal Mastery is about being intentionally prepared for life's challenges and day-to-day life. Self-efficacy is an important part of self-mastery. Self-efficacy is honing your skills, talents, capabilities, abilities, and gifts in a disciplined manner to increase your life effectiveness.

Personal mastery is a commitment to becoming the master of your life skills, talents, gifts, abilities, and capabilities. It is a commitment to continuous discipline, hard work, and paying the price to developing, growing, and reinventing your life potential. Through Personal Mastery, you are stretched, refined, and forged by life's challenges and it helps you to thrive in a volatile, uncertain, complex, and ambiguous world.

Developing Personal Insight and Personal Mastery is an important and intentional self-investment in your life. It is a deliberate lifelong development and growth process to know yourself better each day. Through this process you can master your strengths to increase your credibility and to leverage them to create an inspiring future.

THE FIRST PRINCIPLES

THE UNSTOPPABLE LIFE MATRIX

The Unstoppable Life Matrix describes four quadrants of living a purposeful and Unstoppable Life.

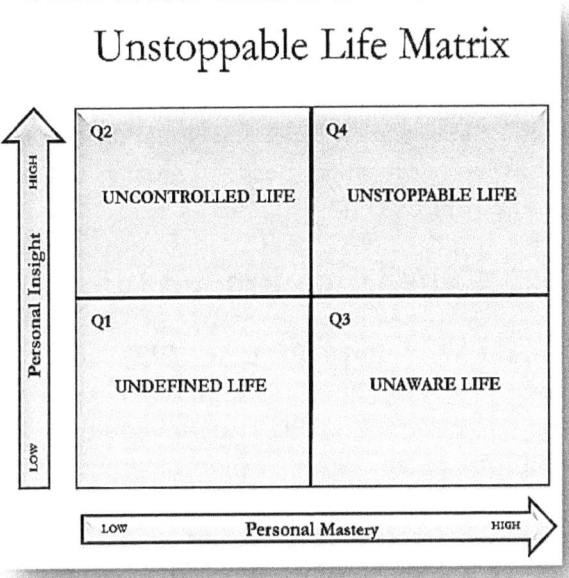

The vertical axis measures your personal insight and self-awareness. The horizontal axis measures the degree of personal mastery or self-control you have in your life.

As you move along the four quadrants of the matrix, you move from being lost in life to surviving and on to a thriving and Unstoppable Life. This life is realized through continuous growth, continuous development, and constantly reinventing yourself.

The Undefined Life

Quadrant 1 (Low PI/Low PM) this is the Undefined Life quadrant and is characterized by uncertainty and ambiguity. This is a person with low personal mastery coupled with a low degree of personal insight or awareness. This is a person living an uninspired, indecisive, and directionless life. Life without direction is useless. This person lacks a personal vision for their life, has no established personal goals, and lacks a disciplined approach to living life.

The Uncontrolled Life

Quadrant 2 (High PI/Low PM) this is the Uncontrolled Life quadrant and is characterized by strong self-awareness and lack of self-control. This is a person with a high degree of personal insight and self-awareness but a low degree of self-control and personal mastery. This person understands who they are and understands their purpose in life but lacks the self-mastery to live an unstoppable life. They do not have a disciplined approach to life development, lack control of their life, and allow outside influences to control their outcomes.

The Unaware Life

Quadrant 3 (Low PI/High PM) this is the Unaware Life quadrant and is characterized by strong self-control coupled with lack of personal insight or incomplete understanding of their full capability. This is a person with a high degree of self-control and personal mastery coupled with a low degree of personal insight or self-awareness. This person understands their capabilities and abilities but lacks a personal vision, purpose, and character development. They do not have a disciplined approach to self-discovery and reflection.

The Unstoppable Life

Quadrant 4 (High PI/High PM) this is the Unstoppable Life quadrant and is characterized by strong self-mastery and strong personal insight. This person has a disciplined approach to living life. This is a person with a high degree of self-control and personal mastery coupled with a high degree of personal insight or self-awareness. This person understands their capabilities and abilities and has a well-defined personal vision, purpose, and character development. They have a disciplined approach to self-discovery and reflection.

Living in Quadrant 4

Anything is possible when you choose to believe in yourself, your life's purpose, and your talents, skills, and abilities. Your life purpose unleashes you to live your life and allows you to be unstoppable. Your greatest power in life is the liberty to choose. It is the liberty to choose what you want to do with your life, where you want to go, and what you want to become.

No one can take this power away from you; it is yours alone. You can do what you want to do; you can be who you want to be. You can live an empowered life through your decisions and choices each day. Your choices determine your attitude and your altitude. When you follow a strong and empowering purpose, you will be Unstoppable.

SUMMARY

The first real mark of becoming an Unstoppable Leader is through self-awareness. Being an Unstoppable Leader is a mindset. It is an unwavering belief in yourself, your abilities, and your capabilities. It is a belief in your unshakeable purpose and values.

You have to believe in yourself with conviction and commitment. It is an awareness of your strengths and your challenges. It is about self-efficacy, self-awareness, and intentional clarity. Once you have recognized your purpose and values and ingrained them, you begin to shape your Unstoppable Leadership.

CHARACTER CHECK

1. Do you understand your talents, skills, and strengths?

2. Are you aware of your leadership drivers?

3. Where are you on the Unstoppable Matrix?

LOOKING INTO THE MIRROR

After reading this chapter, review and reflect on the ideas and concepts presented. Think about what opportunities, challenges, resources, or blind spots you may encounter when you begin your growth and development journey.

Use the following questions to help you grow and develop.

1. How will I incorporate this principle into my leadership development?

2. What opportunity and resources exist for me to use this principle this week, this year?

3. What blind spots may derail me from using this principle?

COMMITMENT TIME

- ✓ The beginning of Unstoppable Leadership starts with self-awareness and self-leadership

- ✓ Self-awareness is understanding and discovering your purpose and is the key to your success as a leader

- ✓ You must want to change and reinvent yourself

- ✓ Know yourself…first

- ✓ Understand how you see the world and your leadership lens

- ✓ You are responsible for discovering your life purpose

- ✓ Take time to discover who you really are

- ✓ Seek to understand yourself before you seek to understand others

- ✓ Find your passionate purpose

- ✓ Knowing yourself makes you more effective in your organization, with teams and with others

- ✓ Your purpose provides you context and focus for your life

LEADERSHIP NOTES

CHAPTER THREE

THE AUTHENTICITY PRINCIPLE

LEADING WITH THE REAL YOU

"Try not to become a person of success, but rather try to become a person of value."
Albert Einstein

I grew up in a military family. My grandfather, father, uncles, aunt, and cousins served as enlisted personnel in all four military services. They felt it was one's duty and an honor to serve their Country. My family served during World War II, the Korean Conflict, the Vietnam War, and the Gulf War.

It was through the example of their Selfless Service that I first learned about the value and importance of the 7Cs--Character, Competence, Courage, Commitment, Communication, Connections, and Choices. It was through their example that I chose to serve in the Air Force and why the 7Cs are the underlying foundation of Unstoppable Leadership. It was during Basic Military Training (BMT) that the 7Cs lesson began to unfold.

One of the first things they provide you at BMT is the big book of success--the training manual. Inside this book was everything you needed to know in order to graduate from BMT and be successful in the Air Force.

The book established the expectations and standards for a successful career. It specified the roles and responsibilities for each rank and it explained the significance of each core value. The book gave you a road map to succeed in the Air Force and the 7Cs were the key and the compass to navigate the map.

The next book of success was AFI 36-2618, *The Enlisted Force Structure*. This book established the criteria for leadership and development levels and responsibilities. AFI 36-2618 gave you a path to be a successful leader and subject matter expert. It gave you the knowledge and understanding of what was expected of you at each level of responsibility and career level. Again, the 7Cs was the major theme in my development.

Finally, as I grew and developed as a leader the 7Cs became a permanent part of my daily life. The overall leadership lesson I learned over the years is that my character is the sum total of my inner core—my values, beliefs, and worldview—and it drives and shapes my behaviors, choices, and actions as a leader.

THE IMPORTANCE OF THE 7CS

In the previous chapter, I talked about the Inner Core and its importance. Your inner core influences how you operate in the world. Your values, beliefs, and worldview influence your priorities, decisions, actions, and your behavior. The foundations of Unstoppable Leadership are the 7Cs--Character, Competence, Courage, Commitment, Communication, Connections, and Choices.

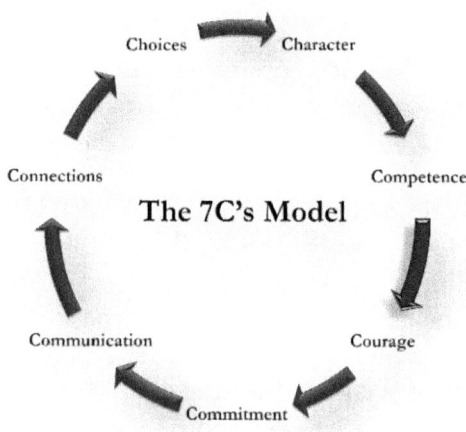

The 7C's Model

Through the influence of your inner core you become an Unstoppable Leader. The heart and soul of Unstoppable Leadership is making the choice to have the courage and commitment to develop your character and competence each day. Leading with your purpose and your core values ensures your life and leadership are congruent.

Your leadership journey begins when you understand your purpose, values, beliefs, and then lead yourself consciously and deliberately with this knowledge. You must fully understand who you are, what you can do, and what you can offer before you can lead others effectively and efficiently.

CHARACTER

"The only person you are destined to become is the person you decide to be."
Ralph Waldo Emerson

Authentic Character drives your leadership. People will follow a leader that they trust and are true to their character. Character is a key part of the unstoppable inner core, shaped by your purpose, values, beliefs, and worldview, and manifested in your character authenticity, integrity, trust, and credibility.

When your character and competence are continuously developed and honed, it gives you the self-confidence, courage, and commitment to lead others. When you are fully committed to leading others and delivering on your promises and commitments, then you solidify your leadership credibility and trustworthiness.

Character plays a vital role in your life and leadership. It is integral to honest leadership and is the difference between success and failure. The Air Force core values of Integrity First, Service Before Self, and Excellence in All We Do established a core foundation for building my character and establishing my leadership expectations.

They helped to set the standard for leadership and my character. The key leadership lesson in character is--living your core values every day is an important aspect of your character in action.

No matter your competence, courage, commitment, or even rank, if you sacrifice your integrity, you sacrifice your trustworthiness as a leader. The foundation of trust is found in the integrity of your leadership.

COMPETENCE

Competence plays a vital role in your technical expertise. Competence is a measure of your level of ability and expertise. It defines your technical expectations and helps you define what talents, abilities, capabilities, and skills you need to be the expert.

The more competent you become, the more others trust in your expertise and ability. Competence is the mastery of your abilities, skills, talents, aptitudes, and capabilities. To maintain your competence level you must commit to lifelong development and growth.

Your competence must be grown, developed, and honed each day of your life. Competence must be constantly honed to keep your leadership edge. Leadership skills and talents atrophy when not used consistently or improved upon. You need to continuously develop your competence.

The more competent you become, the more others trust in your expertise and ability. Your level of mastery is determined by the quantity and quality of hard work you put in to education, experience, development, and learning. Continuous learning helps you stay competitive by developing new capabilities and skills.

The key leadership lesson in competence is--you need to know your strengths and weaknesses and know what kind of expertise you will need to learn to remain proficient and effective. Pursuing mastery and continuing to grow, develop, and reinvent yourself empowers you for greater leadership roles and responsibilities.

You must be passionate about growing, developing, and reinventing yourself to hone your competence to a fine edge. Your level of competence directly relates to your ability to influence your team or organization.

COURAGE

Courage is not the absence of fear, but the willingness, ability, and commitment to act in the face of your fears. It is getting out of your comfort zone and taking the risk to lead and live greatly. It takes a lot of inner strength to do what you think is right even though it may not be easy. It takes courage to sacrifice for those you lead each day.

Courage demands great strength and at times great sacrifice--physically, mentally, and morally. Physical courage utilizes the strength of your body for the act of bravery. Mental courage utilizes the strength of your mind to fortify you for an act of bravery.

You must display personal and moral courage daily. It takes daily courage to lead yourself and people. It takes courage to be authentic, to live out your values, and to inspire people. Being accountable means you are fully responsible for the assigned task, job, or project and responsible for its success or failure based on your actions.

The key leadership lesson in courage is--you need to set and enforce the standards daily and be the living example for your people every day. You are accountable and responsible for taking care of your people and mission accomplishment. Being a leader means taking the moral high ground and standing up for your beliefs and values while risking alienation and ridicule by those who do not agree with you. You must have the courage to lead each day despite the challenges.

Physical and mental courage enables you to act in the face of danger, personal risk, or to overcome fear and complete your task or mission. Moral courage gives you the strength you need to stand firm in your convictions. It is also the willingness to take the negative consequences of an unpopular action. Courage is a leadership essential.

COMMITMENT

Commitment is your unyielding choice to be responsible and accountable for your life, your choices, your character, and your competence. Commitment is your ability to hold yourself accountable and to remain resolute in your convictions. Commitment allows you to keep your character intact during trials and challenges and builds trust, credibility, and respect through your commitment to live by standards and principles.

You must be committed to your team and organization to lead effectively. You must be committed to inspiring and motivating your team every day. You must be committed to aligning your core values with your organization's core values in order to lead from the front.

The key leadership lesson in commitment is--as a leader of a team or organization, your people will watch to see if you are committed to living the core values and living the standard, and then they will follow your lead. Commitment shows in your attitude and actions and by being personally dedicated to organizational goals and values.

COMMUNICATION

A leader must be able to communicate effectively. A leader must master one-on-one and enterprise communication capabilities in order to effectively influence and inspire. Unstoppable Leaders must be strong communicators.

A leader must understand that:

- Communication is vital to leadership and moving organizations forward

- Ambiguity can be reduced through clear and precise communication

- Develop your communication skill as you develop your leadership skills

- Clear communication helps to build solid teams and alliances

A lack of communication breeds distrust among team members. Developing communication skills is essential to being an effective leader and displaying effective leadership. Communication skills like speaking, writing, and listening are essential leadership abilities. These skills allow a leader to transfer their message, listen for feedback, and establish a dialogue with their team.

The key leadership lesson in communication is--if you cannot get your message across to each team member, then your ability to influence, motivate, and inspire your team to action is diminished. When leaders communicate with clarity and purposefully, team members choose to follow them.

People stay with companies that inspire, motivate, and communicate with them. People want to feel a part of something that is important and will make a difference. Communication allows a leader to inspire, encourage, and make all people feel a part of the team.

CONNECTIONS

All leadership is about building and maintaining relationships or connections. Without people there is no leadership. Connecting with other people, as individuals and at the personal level, is the key to leading them. When you connect with people at the personal level, you show them that you respect them as individuals and for who they are. You connect with them at the heart and soul level.

I have had the opportunity to interact with Bellevue University coaches and listen to them talk about how they recruit new players each year. The struggle is not locating talent, it is trying to connect with them during the recruitment visit.

Connecting and building trust with a new recruit and their family is one of the most important skills needed by the coaches. Connecting and building trust starts with the coach taking the first step in recognizing the player's talent, but more importantly, the player as an individual.

It also starts by the coach recognizing the importance of the family and its tie to the player. The coach starts building the connection by offering and extending trust first.

Connecting and building the trust relationship can be the difference between a successful recruiting trip or coming home empty-handed.

The key leadership lesson in connections is--people no longer want to be managed or motivated, they want to be inspired and desire a sense of purpose when they work. As a leader, you need to connect at a heart, mind, body, and soul level in order to tap into the potential of your people.

A leader needs to be able to build relationships with all people inside and outside the organization. A leader needs to understand that a good team needs direction and growth to become a truly great team.

CHOICES

Everything you do to be successful is based on your decisions, choices, and actions--you are responsible and accountable for your choices and decisions. It is by choice, not by chance, that you will determine your life. Your choices play an important and powerful role in your life and leadership. All leadership begins and ends with a choice.

Your destiny and career is determined by the choices you make. Your decisions are the single most important factor that drives your life.

Your decisions are the A.I.R. (Action, Impact, and Result) or the breath of life you take each day to live. Each decision is made from your action, the impact of the action, and the results of that action.

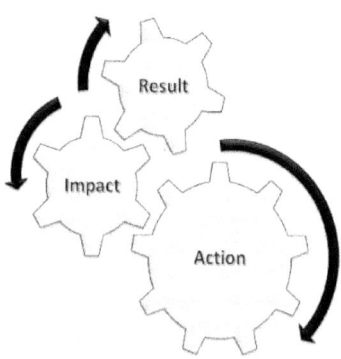

As a leader, you will make decisions and choices in the course of your day. You need to understand the kinetic effect of your decisions and the direct and indirect effect they will have on you and your team.

The key leadership lesson in choices begins with you taking responsibility and accountability for your choices. Each day you choose to believe in yourself, your abilities, your courage to act, and your daily direction.

As a leader, your decisions and choices have significant consequences in your life and leadership. At times, being the leader requires that you make unpopular decisions for the right reasons.

LEADING FROM THE SWEET SPOT

A synergy, or Sweet Spot, develops when your inner core and your Character, Competence, Courage, Commitment, Communication, Connections, and Choices are used together to lead and influence others.

Leading from the Sweet Spot means your inner core is aligned with the 7Cs and drives how you live your life. This convergence of your inner core and the 7Cs allows you to lead by be design and not by chance.

Why is leading from the Sweet Spot important? When you have learned to lead your own life, then you have a solid foundation from which you can effectively lead others. If you have not mastered leading yourself, then your words, actions, behaviors, and decisions will not be congruent with your inner core.

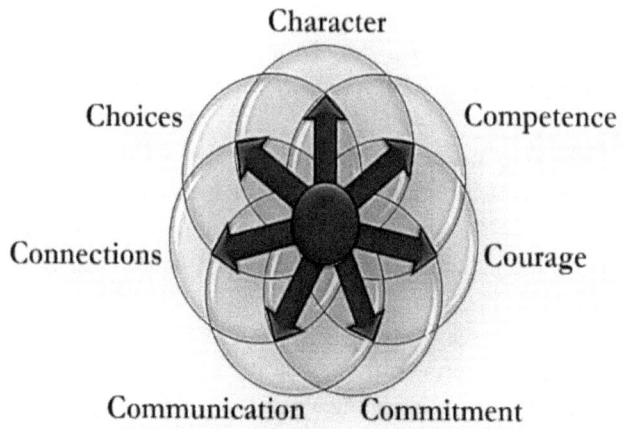

Leading from the Sweet Spot means your actions and behavior must align with one another in order for you to make an impact on your team and organization. Through your words and actions, you lead by example and live out the culture you want your team and organization to follow.

Leading from the Sweet Spot means you have mastered the art of self-insight and self-mastery and truly know who you are as a leader. You must be able to lead your life through Personal Insight and Personal Mastery in order to achieve your desired end state and life goals.

Leading from the Sweet Spot means your leadership drivers, your character, your attitude, and your thinking are in tune with each other and you have inner core synergy.

THE FIRST PRINCIPLES

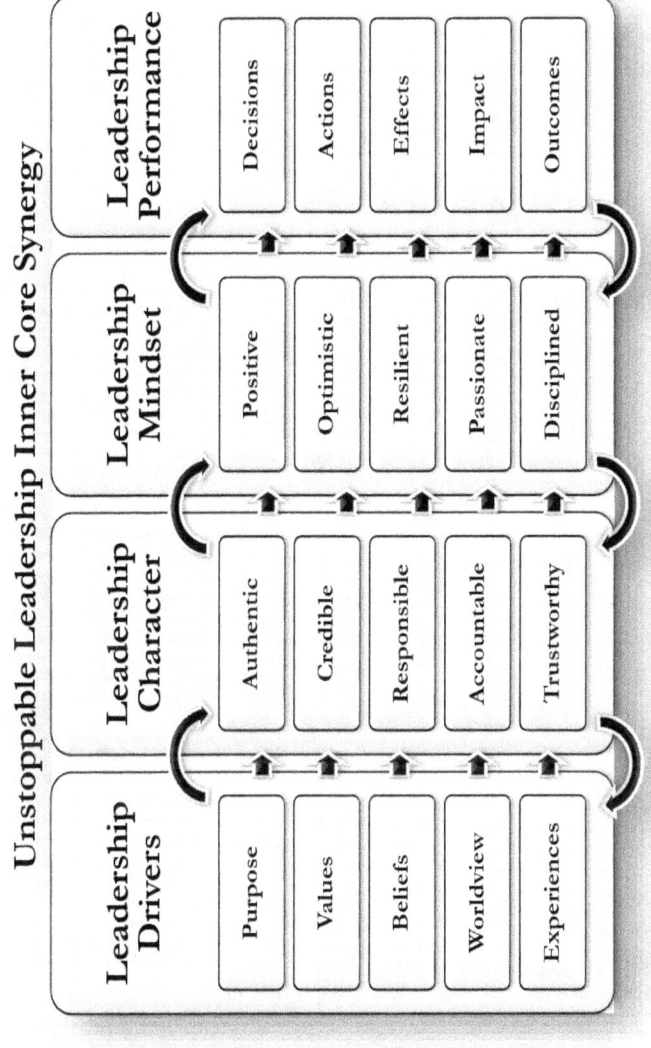

LEADERSHIP CHARACTER

As a leader, you set the tone and mood of your team culture and work environment. Leading by example is the most important thing. In your professional life and in your private life, if people do not believe in you, they won't trust you. You begin building your credibility by exploring your inner core.

You earn and maintain your credibility by clarifying your values, beliefs, and worldview. By truly understanding these three items you will understand how you make decisions and take action as a leader. Leadership is your character on display for everyone to see. Every blemish, every flaw, and every fault will be seen unless you mold and shape your character daily.

The stresses and challenges of leadership will also reveal what your character is made of. Unstoppable Leadership is not about power, position, or personality, it is about the realization that who you are inside, what your character is made of, is who you will be as a leader.

Unstoppable Leadership is having the integrity to be authentic as a leader. Your honor, integrity, and authenticity are foundational to Unstoppable Leadership.

Leader credibility, organizational trust, and respect begin with a solid foundation of accountability and responsibility. Your leadership character is everything to being a leader. You must embrace the fact that your leadership drivers shape your character.

Living and leading with character is living and leading with authenticity. Authentic character is directly related to your credibility, trustworthiness, and reliability.

Being authentic is being the genuine you, the real deal, no falsehoods, no acting, no pretending, and no wearing a mask, just the true you. Your team does not observe your character, values, or beliefs, they observe only your day-to-day behavior.

INTEGRITY

Leadership is about building trust and having integrity. Integrity is key to building and sustaining your character. Your integrity is more than just a character trait. It is your most precious leadership resource and is an essential personal and professional life trait.

Integrity is the cornerstone of a leader's character. It is the stamp of an authentic leader. Integrity must remain intact or a leader loses credibility and becomes untrustworthy.

Character begins with your inner core. Defining your character begins by reflecting on who you are and seeing if your actions reflect positively on you as a person of character.

It is the willingness to do what is right even when no one is looking. It is the "moral compass"--the inner voice; the voice of self-control; the basis for the trust imperative in today's world.

THE FIRST PRINCIPLES

Being a leader is about authentic character and integrity. Leadership is about building, maintaining, and cultivating trust with your team or across an organization. Trust is the glue that keeps teams and organizations successful.

Being a leader of integrity requires a conscious decision to live and lead with honor and authenticity. The word integrity originates from the Latin *integer* meaning whole, complete, or undivided. The Merriam-Webster dictionary further defines integrity as following a strong moral code. Integrity refines and defines your character each day.

You cannot survive if you lack integrity or wholeness. A lack of integrity will cause a tension or conflict in your life until you realign yourself to your purpose, values, and beliefs. Integrity means living by your word, keeping your promises, and over-delivering in everything you do.

To be truly authentic, your words and actions need to be the same. Integrity is the cornerstone of leadership trust. Trust strengthens a leader's influence and credibility.

Integrity involves character authenticity, reliability, credibility, and trustworthiness. Living with integrity requires a concerted effort on your part to live authentically and congruent to your values each day. However, despite your hard work, your integrity can be lost in a momentary lapse of reasoning. Integrity means that you are willing to live an authentic and true life.

AUTHENTIC

Several years ago I bought an Eagle in Flight sculpture for my office and it came with a Certificate of Authenticity from the artist. He personally signed the certificate and guaranteed this was a genuine original and authentic piece of his artwork and not a replica, or copy. By personally signing the certificate, he was staking his character, credibility, and trustworthiness as an artist and businessperson for all to see.

What if each leader had a Certificate of Authenticity attached to them so everyone could see that they were the "Genuine Article" and not a false leader? The real question for you is, if you had a Certificate of Authenticity attached to your leadership, would you stake your character, credibility, and trustworthiness by signing it?

Today, more than ever, people want authenticity. They look for authenticity in the products they buy. They look for it in the foods they eat. But most of all, they look for it in their leaders. They want leaders who are honest, credible, and reliable. They want leaders who have integrity, are responsible, and are accountable.

They want leaders who are committed to connect and communicate with them as real people and not just employees. They want leaders who are real and are the "Genuine Article". Authenticity means a person is accountable and responsible for their actions, words, and decisions.

Integrity is the trust factor in life. Integrity is the consequence of setting and maintaining high standards, honorable practices, virtuous ways, and moral actions. Authentic integrity allows your character to stand the test of time and challenges. Integrity in your life means that you intend to live an authentic and true life. You cannot survive if you lack integrity or wholeness.

Authenticity is about being the real you and not being afraid to live out your inner core. Authenticity is being a genuine leader and living your unstoppable inner core--your values, beliefs, and worldview.

Awareness is the deep dive of Discovery while Authenticity is having the courage and commitment to live out your discoveries. Authenticity means you are accountable and responsible for your actions, words, and decisions. Being an Unstoppable Leader is being who you really are--honest and unafraid.

In Shakespeare's play *Hamlet*, Polonius is providing advice to Laertes, *"And this above all, to thine own self be true. Then, it must follow as the night the day, thou canst not then be false to any man."* This is critical for you to understand as a leader--your leadership is always under scrutiny by your people.

THE IMPORTANCE OF AUTHENTICITY

One of the main things I learned in the military and in life is that your life and leadership are what you make of them and you are responsible and accountable for what you create. A good example of why authenticity is important is in a life story below.

In December 1997, we moved from Tucson, Arizona, to Bitburg, Germany. We looked at the new assignment as a new adventure and new family opportunity to see more of the world. As part of that new adventure we booked a family tour called Three Countries which toured Switzerland, Liechtenstein, and Austria. During the tour, we visited Sursee and Lucerne, Switzerland; Vaduz, Liechtenstein; and Feldkirch, Austria.

The tour was a great way to start our new assignment and family adventure. Everything was going as the tour operator planned until we reached the Austrian border. As our bus prepared to cross from Liechtenstein to Austria, the Austrian Polizei were stopping every car, truck, and bus as part of a checkpoint search to check for proper identification and contraband.

As our bus reached the checkpoint, the Polizei stopped the bus and entered and asked everyone to pull out their passports and IDs. After they realized that the bus carried US Military personnel, they ordered all military personnel off the bus. We lined up along the side of the bus, each person was asked to produce their military IDs and traveling authorization papers. The IDs were looked over, each name checked against the bus manifest, and each person compared to their ID photo.

After a quite lengthy process of checking to see if our military identification was authentic or forgeries, the Austrian Polizei took all the IDs and went back to the border crossing office. Finally, after leaving us to stand outside the bus for an hour, the Polizei walked back to the bus and we were released. That border incident taught me a lot about the importance of genuineness and authenticity.

Authenticity means you must be your true self and live a genuine and congruent life in order to be an Unstoppable Leader. You cannot lead effectively if you lack personal integrity and honesty with your own self. It begins with you first before you can lead others.

A lack of personal integrity will cause tension or conflict in your life until you realign yourself to your purpose, values, and beliefs. **Bottom Line: To thine oneself be true.**

You must take ownership of your authentic life and leadership. Authentic leaders model and maintain their values and act in a way that is both honest and congruent with their beliefs and values.

Authenticity means taking control of your life, living out your purpose, and living unstoppable. Being authentic is being the same person at home, at the office, at church, or in the community--congruent character. In addition, when you live a lie, you lead from that same lie, and your true leadership is inauthentic.

TRUSTWORTHY

A vital component of a leader's success is trust and is the very heart of a leader-follower relationship. A trustworthy leader builds a culture of integrity and respect and maintains trust with others. The relationship of the leader and the subordinate is a team relationship built on trust, respect, and integrity.

Trust is essential for the type of creativity and innovation that needs to occur in organizations today. A leader who is open and honest today never has to remember the lie told yesterday. Trust is crucial to leadership. No one wants to follow an untrustworthy leader.

People need to trust, respect, and believe in you. Mutual trust and respect is necessary if you want to live with integrity. You will earn and maintain trust when you hold yourself accountable and responsible as a leader. You can do this by leading with integrity of character, congruent to your core values, and with honesty. Being a person of authenticity and integrity is a conscious decision. Integrity is key to building and sustaining trust.

Trust and respect begins with a solid foundation of lifelong integrity and congruency. Leaders who build and maintain trust will build effective and successful teams. How do you build a great team? By leading by example each day. Leading by example is living out your authentic leadership through actions and not just words.

Your walk and talk must be congruent. There is no falsehood in your leadership, just integrity of character and purpose. In the end, your actions are the driving force that influences your team. You must set the tone and lead by example.

An Unstoppable Leader leads by example. A trustworthy leader builds a culture of integrity and respect and maintains trust with others.

When you fail to live authentically and by example, you have failed as a leader to live up to the trust and credibility that your people have granted you. Because of your lack of integrity you have broken the trust bond with your people. You are accountable and responsible for your people and the success of your team.

You need to understand how to build and maintain trust, keep your integrity, and continue to build your credibility. Trust is a relationship established between you and another person.

In each relationship, you take a risk when you trust another person. You are taking a risk that the other person is trustworthy. When you build your relationships on integrity, respect, and trust, you are relying on that risk and letting the other person know that they are trustworthy.

RELIABLE

Unstoppable Leaders model and maintain the values of the organization and act in a way that is both honest and trusting. A leader positively influences the moral element of an organization and determines the outcome of situations.

A reliable leader demonstrates the capability to act in an influential, urgent, and steadfast way to realize outcomes and results. They remain focused on the organizational goals and leverage all available resources to achieve that goal. Reliability is revealed through your consistent actions over time.

CREDIBILITY

Credibility comes from personal expertise and knowing what you are doing. It also relates to the results that are likely to occur through your actions. A leader must be able to improvise, adapt, and overcome as rapidly as the current pace of change.

You begin building your credibility by exploring your inner core--your character, competence, courage, and commitment. You earn and maintain your credibility by clarifying your values, beliefs, and worldview. Credibility is the belief factor in your leadership.

If you are credible and competent, people will believe in you and follow your lead because they trust you. The surest way for you to lose your credibility is by failing to take responsibility for your actions, decisions, and mistakes. Your credibility crumbles when your words and actions appear inconsistent with your core values and your character. Your authentic character makes a difference every day in the lives of others.

Without a solid character foundation, the critical link of trust between leaders and followers will not exist. As a credible and authentic leader, your personal honor and integrity should be at the very center of your core. Respect is a key component of credibility. Your ability to extend respect to all people is vital to your success as a leader and gaining the respect of others is necessary for the success of your leadership.

Trust and respect are preconditions for open communication and authentic dialogue. Unstoppable Leaders treat people with dignity and respect and demonstrate the character, courage, competence, and commitment that build trust.

A CULTURE OF INTEGRITY

Why are honor, integrity, and authenticity important for you as a leader? People need to trust, respect, and believe in you. Mutual trust and respect is necessary if you want to live with integrity. Have you ever played the game of JENGA?

The goal of the game is for alternating players to remove a block from the middle or lower levels of the tower and place it on the top level of the tower until the tower falls over from critical instability. The winner is the one who last completed a level successfully.

If you step back for a moment and look at your life and leadership, how often do you do that same JENGA process with your life?

- You sacrifice values and beliefs in order to fit in at work

- You sacrifice values and beliefs to fit in with your peers

- You sacrifice values and beliefs for profit
- You sacrifice values and beliefs for a promotion
- You sacrifice and sacrifice until the tower topples and your character and integrity are compromised

When you create a culture of honor, trust, respect, and integrity, you establish a culture of trustworthiness. When you create an environment of integrity, honor, trust, and respect, you enlarge, empower, and value each person.

It is all about building and sustaining relationships. Authenticity means a leader is accountable and responsible for their actions, words, and decisions. You need to create a culture that cultivates accountability and responsibility. You must be committed to leading with daily personal and professional honor, accountability, and trust.

LEADERSHIP INSIGHT

Without leadership authenticity and accountability, team and organizational trust disappears, the critical link of trust between the leader and team will not exist, and leadership effectiveness fails. Integrity in your life means that you intend to live an authentic and true life. Through your words and actions you create the culture of integrity you want your team and the organization to follow.

When your words and actions are not congruent, then the organization will have a culture of disbelief and untrustworthiness. Behavior and culture must align with one another in order for change to happen.

As a leader, you must make sure you do not live by two sets of values, one for yourself, and one for your people. Authenticity cannot be words that come out of your mouth, you must live authentically each day. **You must constantly deliver on your promises, live up to your commitments, and display value congruency to your team.** By living and leading authentically, you guarantee your people that you are a real and genuine leader every day of the week not just Monday through Friday.

As a leader of honor and integrity you must lead by example and be true to your values. When you hold yourself accountable and responsible, it becomes a powerful inspirational motivator for your team. It will motivate them to adopt and live a similar lifestyle.

The ethos of accountability and responsibility starts with you actively making it your day-to-day goal to be accountable and responsible. You are in direct contact on a daily basis with your team and influence and affect their lives.

The best way that you can show accountability and responsibility is by being a role model. As an Unstoppable Leader, you should strive to lead by example to reinforce your leadership authenticity and to have your team want to emulate your daily walk.

In addition, relationships are built upon trust and respect which is all about your character. Integrity means living by your word, keeping your promises, and over-delivering in everything you do. An Unstoppable Leader seeks to lead their teams and their organizations authentically and with integrity.

To be truly authentic, your words and actions need to be the same. You need to be responsible for your thoughts, feelings, words, and actions.

Unstoppable Leaders are vital to today's organizations. Today, the workplace is reliant on trust. A key to success with your team and organization is that you are credible and trustworthy. Your character will determine if your leadership is successful and if it will stand the test of time. When you lead with your inner core and your authentic character, you inspire your team and you motivate them to accomplish the mission.

Word of Caution: do not be a Popeye leader and exclaim to everyone, "I am what I am so accept me for who I am." What you are telling everyone is that you are unwilling to grow, develop, or reinvent yourself as a leader. Do not be surprised if members of your team start to leave.

WHY, WHAT, AND HOW

A key tool for you to use to ensure you lead by example with integrity is to write it down in a vision and mission statement. You need to make it a visible part of your daily life. Personal vision and mission statements bring clarity and focus to your leadership.

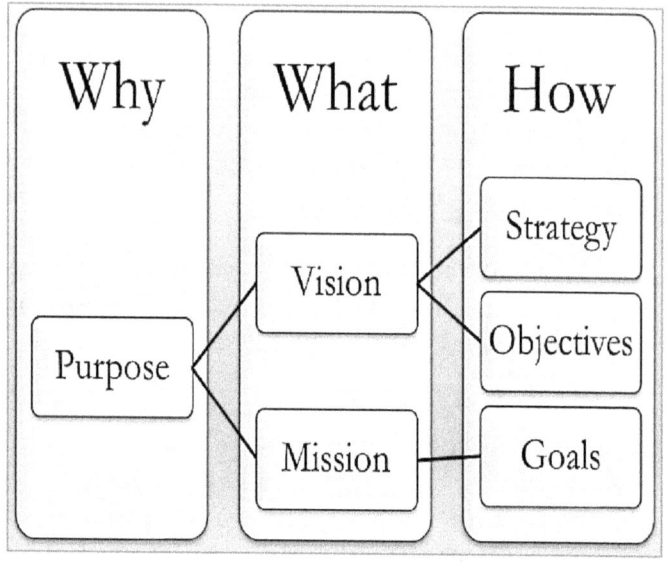

Your life purpose answers the question of "why" you are here. It is your reason for being and leading. A vision statement isolates "what you want to accomplish" while you are here. A mission statement specifies "the method" you want to use to accomplish your purpose.

A vision is a rich, vivid, and captivating mental picture of the life you want to create. It should excite and motivate you to live. Your personal vision statement is a strategic or "big picture" view of your life. The first person you need to inspire is yourself.

A personal vision statement is a vision of whom you want to become. After you develop your vision, your next step is to translate your purpose and vision into a personal mission statement.

Your personal mission statement is what you plan to do to achieve your vision. Writing your mission statement begins by focusing on your values, your life's philosophy, your purpose, talents, skills, and your guiding principles. A personal mission statement is not a one-time event, but an evolving process.

As you grow and develop as a person, your mission statement will change. Your mission statement crystallizes your life. As you continue to develop yourself and your purpose, you need a way to inspire and focus yourself along your journey.

The vision and mission statements help you to implement your well-defined life and leadership goals. Having a personal vision and mission statement is a tangible method to writing down your vision, purpose, and long-term and short-term life goals.

Goals refer to "how you plan to accomplish" specific goals to the actions and results needed to complete your mission and realize your purpose. It is about moving from the "as-is" life to the "to-be" life.

VISION AND MISSION

Life and leadership begins with a clear picture and a vision to fulfill your purpose. Every leader needs a vision to establish a direction and a plan to get there. Your leadership vision provides the inspiration and the passion for accomplishing your leadership purpose. Be bold and stretch your leadership when defining your vision.

- What do you see yourself doing or your team accomplishing over the next 6 months, year, or 3 years?

- How do you plan to get there?

- Who is going with you?

- How does your vision fulfill your leadership purpose?

As you continue to develop your vision and define your leadership purpose, you need a way to inspire and focus yourself along your journey. This statement is for you to use as a constant reminder of where you are going in life and what is important. The leader's vision provides clarity and focus to the organization. A leader must envision and communicate an inspiring vision and clearly define a strategy for the future.

VISION REQUIREMENTS

A real and effective vision, one that paints the picture of the future, should be:

- Inspiring: Each person must have the passion to make the vision a reality; the vision should motivate people to action

- Challenging: The vision must stretch and grow your team; they should be challenged to go beyond doing just enough to get by and want to work even smarter and harder to help make the vision a reality

- Attainable: It should make people want to deliberately move toward the vision; a vision must be focused on the most important things

- Enabling: Your team must feel empowered and energized to make the vision their future; people should be able to see that what they do relates to what the vision describes

- Focused: The vision must be believable and focused on how the organization will need to change; it has to clearly address what it is that will make the organization successful

SUMMARY

Your character is the true essence of who you are as a person and how you lead as a leader. It is the very core of what drives you and influences your actions and reactions. Character defines your authentic leadership.

Each day that you show up to work your people look to see how you lead and live your life. They are looking to see if you are authentic. In fact, it is key and essential to you being a leader. To be an Unstoppable Leader you need to be authentic in your words, conduct, and actions with yourself and others. You need to live out your values and beliefs.

CHARACTER CHECK

1. How authentic are you as a leader?

2. Do you live your values daily?

3. Are you a genuine leader?

LOOKING INTO THE MIRROR

After reading this chapter, review and reflect on the ideas and concepts presented. Think about what opportunities, challenges, resources, or blind spots you may encounter when you begin your growth and development journey.

Use the following questions to help you grow and develop.

1. How will I incorporate this principle into my leadership development?

2. What opportunity and resources exist for me to use this principle this week, this year?

3. What blind spots may derail me from using this principle?

COMMITMENT TIME

- ✓ Lead with authenticity and integrity
- ✓ Character authenticity is living on purpose
- ✓ You are the owner of your successes, failures, emotions, and feelings
- ✓ Character authenticity means being the very best leader you can be
- ✓ Be authentic in your words and actions
- ✓ Let your values be an important part of the foundation for the development of your vision
- ✓ Refuse to compromise your character
- ✓ Live your life with integrity
- ✓ Refuse to compromise your values
- ✓ Refuse to compromise your beliefs
- ✓ Leading with integrity is a conscious decision
- ✓ Integrity is more than just a character trait, it is an essential life trait
- ✓ Integrity in your life means that you intend to live an authentic and true life

THE FIRST PRINCIPLES

LEADERSHIP NOTES

CHAPTER FOUR

THE COURAGE PRINCIPLE

LEADING WITH COURAGE AND AUDACITY

"Courage is doing what you're afraid to do. There can be no courage unless you're scared."
Eddie Rickenbacker

When General John Reynolds was killed in the first day's fighting at Gettysburg, Major General Winfield Scott Hancock took charge on the battlefield. He recommended to General George Meade that the Union Army continue the fight at Gettysburg.

It was he that selected the ground on which the army deployed to fight for the second and third day. Major General Hancock knew that his presence on the battlefield would encourage and embolden his soldiers to stand fast and fight because he was with them through the thick of the fighting.

Hancock directed the action in the Union center until wounded. General Hancock led from the front with Courageous Leadership and by doing so inspired his troops to greatness during Pickett's Charge on the third day of the Gettysburg Battle.

When Colonel Curlett and I deployed to the Middle East, we would convoy to Camp Bucca, Iraq, to conduct "outside the wire" missions with our Security Forces Airmen.

During the Area Surveillance Operations and IED sweep missions, we traveled and walked shoulder-to-shoulder with our Airmen looking for command detonation wires, unnatural earthworks, or recent changes in the shoulder areas of the road where an IED could be placed.

We both believed in leadership by example. We both had the same concept of Courageous Leadership. If you want to really inspire Airmen, you need to know your Airmen. You need to understand the Airmen's mission, feel their pain, and most of all see the sense of pride they have doing the mission.

We learned more about Courageous Leadership from the Security Forces Airmen who conducted that mission every day.

They put their lives on the line daily to ensure convoys passed safely. These Combat Airmen had Courageous Leadership that inspired us every time we went on a mission with them.

COURAGEOUS LEADERSHIP

Long-term unpredictability and uncertainty makes courageous leadership essential in today's organizations. Your team needs to see you lead from the front and to inspire them daily toward mission accomplishment.

You were meant to be a courageous leader and live your life courageously. Courage is the foundation and the backbone of your Unstoppable Leadership. Courage is deciding to live authentically, lead boldly, lead confidently, and with integrity. Courage is deciding to lead with your inner core and the strength of your character.

Courageous leadership is leading by example each day you are a leader. Courageous leadership is aligning your values with an organization's values so you lead with synergy and lead powerfully. A courageous leader must have the ability to make the tough moral decisions in daily situations, even when it may not be popular.

It takes courage to decide to do what's right and not necessarily what feels good and what is fun at the time. Courageous leadership is about your leadership integrity and honor.

Integrity is the cornerstone of all leadership actions, for without it there is no trust in the leader, no confidence in their actions, no credibility in their actions, and their words have no meaning. Without integrity, your leadership and your character are hollow and void of real substance.

Where does a leader's courage come from? Courage comes from within. It is the spark that creates your willingness to stand up for what is right and for what you believe in. Courage is powerful and defines your success as a leader. Courage is the lion's roar that gives you the confidence to say, "let's make it happen" and then steels your commitment to charge headlong to make it happen.

Leadership requires personal and professional courage. It requires courage to lead in the good times and the bad times, it requires courage to make the hard choices along with the easy ones.

It requires courage to accept the responsibility for the good and bad results. It requires courage to accept the responsibility for your leadership successes and the failures. If you do not have courage, you will never succeed and win as a leader.

Remember: courage is not the absence of fear, but the willingness and ability to act in the face of your fears and be the bold leader you need to be. True leadership courage involves a focused mindset and an inner conviction to face your challenges, problems, uncertainties, threats, and risks.

General William T. Sherman defines Courage as, "a perfect sensibility of the measure of danger and a mental willingness to endure it." Merriam-Webster's Dictionary describes Courage as the capability to do what needs to be done, regardless of the cost or risk.

COURAGE FOR THE CHALLENGE

Unstoppable Leaders must have the courage to deal with the challenges of volatility, uncertainty, complexity, and ambiguity. A courageous leader can meet and adapt to new challenges, build strategic partnerships, build and sustain human capital organizations, and have the courage to act and react to the challenges.

Physical courage utilizes the strength of your body for the act of bravery. Mental courage utilizes the strength of your mind to fortify you for an act of bravery. Moral courage means taking the moral high ground and standing up for your beliefs and values while risking alienation and ridicule by those who do not agree with you.

All three are important aspects of being courageous. Physical, moral, and mental courage enables you to act in the face of danger, personal risk, or to overcome fear and complete your task or mission.

CHURCHILL ON COURAGE

Prime Minister Winston Churchill was a master communicator and an inspiring speaker. He could motivate people to action and make them believe beyond their own imagination.

On June 4, 1940, Prime Minister Winston Churchill stood before the House of Commons to report on the

Miracle at Dunkirk evacuation and to brace a nation for War. As he spoke about the gallant rescue of the British Expeditionary Forces, he finished up his speech with these words.

> …we shall not flag or fail. We shall go on to the end, we shall fight in France, we shall fight on the seas and oceans, we shall fight with growing confidence and growing strength in the air, we shall defend our Island, whatever the cost may be, we shall fight on the beaches, we shall fight on the landing grounds, we shall fight in the fields and in the streets, we shall fight in the hills; we shall never surrender…

Fourteen days later on June 18, 1940, Prime Minister Churchill once again stood before the House of Commons at the Fall of France on June 17, 1940. Great Britain was now on its own to defend against the assault of Nazi Germany's Blitzkrieg.

> …But if we fail, then the whole world, including the United States, including all that we have known and cared for, will sink into the abyss of a new Dark Age made more sinister, and perhaps more protracted, by the lights of perverted science. Let us therefore brace ourselves to our duties, and so bear ourselves that, if the British Empire and its Commonwealth last for a thousand years, men will still say, 'This was their finest hour.'

Finally, on October 29, 1941, Winston Churchill spoke these words at Harrow School after having survived the first major air war called the Battle of Britain and the massive London Bombings.

> This is the lesson: never give in, never give in, never, never, never, never—in nothing, great or small, large or petty—never give in except to convictions of honour and good sense. Never yield to force; never yield to the apparently overwhelming might of the enemy...There was no flinching and no thought of giving in; and by what seemed almost a miracle to those outside these Islands, though we ourselves never doubted it, we now find ourselves in a position where I say that we can be sure that we have only to persevere to conquer...

CONFIDENCE

Confidence is an ardent belief in yourself, your capabilities, and your ability. Confidence is your greatest personal resource and resilience factor. With confidence you can face life's challenges head on and know that you will survive and thrive. Confidence is indispensable to living an Unstoppable Life.

Confidence is the inner voice that steels you and lets you know you have the capability and the ability to achieve your dreams and goals. There is nothing more powerful than your confidence. It is a life changer. Each act of leadership courage builds your self-confidence as a leader.

Courage is a key factor in developing and maintaining a courageous mindset. To achieve a courageous mindset you must commit yourself to act in a consistent, persistent, and disciplined manner that helps you attain excellence in all you do.

Your moral courage is grounded in your inner core and character. Moral courage allows you to do what you believe is right despite what the world around you says is right.

Moral courage gives you the strength you need to stand firm in your convictions. It is the willingness to take the negative consequences of an unpopular action. Moral courage, even when it is the right thing to do, can mean the loss of friends, reputation, and your job.

Why is moral courage important for a leader? If you lack the moral courage to hold on to your beliefs in the moment of difficulty, peer resistance, or personal opposition, then you lack confidence in yourself and lack a conviction of courage. Your leadership will act just like a sailboat without a main sail and keel. It will ride the waves until it finally capsizes.

COURAGE IS A CHOICE

When you choose to be courageous, your hope, dignity, and inner strength grows stronger. It takes moral courage to decide to do what is right and not necessarily what feels good. Moral courage is setting and living your standards daily and being a role model.

Be an Unstoppable Leader and inspire your team and organization to greatness! Everything you do, whether it is leading yourself, leading a team, or leading in an organization is affected by your commitment to be a courageous leader.

Be committed to being Courageous! Never settle for second best and learn to exceed your own leadership expectations by striving to become the very best leader you can become. If you want to see success in your career, avoid merely meeting expectations.

Exceed the expectations every time you do something. The expectations you exceed today become the seeds for new opportunities in the future. Each day you need the courage to challenge your comfort zone, face your fears, and expand your leadership horizons.

As a leader, you should never remain in a comfort zone. You must be willing to take risks and be bold. Courage also means being able to keep going when the burden is heavy and there is no end in sight. Courage can be the willingness to live one day at a time, doing the best you can.

As an Unstoppable Leader, you must have the courage to forge ahead and blaze a trail forward into unknown and uncharted leadership territory.

- Leaders who take a risk change things
- Leaders who move out of their comfort zones make a difference

- Leaders who lead greatly make an impact on the world

Courage is not simply the absence of fear, but the force of moving forward despite fear. It may be fear of failure, fear of not belonging, or fear of public speaking. There are many types of fears that can attribute to why you do not achieve something or try something new in your life.

BE FEARLESS AND BOLDLY LEAD

To live an Unstoppable Life you need to acknowledge and recognize your fears. Aristotle said that, "…a certain degree of fear is necessary to the formation of true courage. All that is meant here is, that no habit of courage or self-mastery can be said to be matured, until pain altogether vanishes." Your fears can protect you from killing or injuring yourself by doing something reckless or unsafe (i.e., jumping over cars with a motorcycle).

On the other hand, fear can hold you back from realizing your dreams, goals, and living your life. Fear is a ravenous monster that can control your mind and attacks your courage to live fully. It will feed on your anxieties, doubts, worries, uncertainties, and suspicions until it consumes your every thought.

If you do not make it your business to overcome fear, you better believe it will try to overwhelm you. How you develop and train your mind can help you become fearless.

It means you tackle your fear one part at a time, over a period of time. When you are fearless you do not permit your fears to get the better of you, or worse, limit your life. Being fearless means getting out of your comfort zones so you can become unstoppable.

LEADERSHIP STRATEGY

To lead with courage, confidence, and fearlessly you need to know where you are going each day. You need to know the direction you are going and what you want to achieve.

Having a leadership strategy ensures that you have a successful game plan to accomplish your vision and mission. I began to talk about the leadership strategy when we talked about mission and vision statements.

A leadership strategy consists of four key areas:

- Leadership purpose
- Leadership vision and mission statements
- Leadership goals, priorities, and objectives
- Leadership decisions and actions

Your leadership strategy is the foundation and guiding principles of a disciplined approach to being an Unstoppable Leader. Your purpose influences your leadership. Your purpose is the compass that helps you chart your way in the world and in your leadership.

Your life and your leadership are driven by one thing...your purpose in life. Your vision and mission statements are the *where* and *what* of your life strategy. The vision statement is *where* you want to go in life and defines your end state or life outcomes.

Your mission statement is *what* you want to do in the next one, three, five years to move yourself forward to achieving your end states. Your goals, priorities, and objectives are the *how* you want to accomplish your strategy. Your decisions and actions are the *way* you will accomplish your strategy.

GOAL SETTING

Goals provide a sense of accomplishment and achievement. Goal setting begins the process of breaking your vision down into concrete steps. Goals are an indispensable part of effectively leading people and conducting business.

As a leader, you need to take the time to establish long-term and short-term goals for yourself and your team. Intentionality is the bridge between goals and achievement. As an Unstoppable Leader, you consistently achieve the goals you set through passion, perseverance, and persistence.

An intentional and focused leader is resolute and determined to make their goals a reality. Well thought out and concrete goals are what team members will commit to.

DESIGN YOUR STRATEGY: A well-developed leadership strategy clearly defines expectations, responsibilities, performance standards, goals, and objectives. The leadership strategy also assesses the strengths, weaknesses, threats, and opportunities for each individual and the leadership requirements of the organization.

You must set realistic and measurable goals that allow you and your team to stretch your capabilities and achieve the strategies.

Define your goal strategy based on the desired objectives and outcomes. Create strategies and initiatives that allow others to achieve the vision and accomplish current and future challenges and opportunities. Implement your strategy to produce the effects your organization needs.

ESTABLISH YOUR GOALS: Establish clear and S.M.A.R^2.T. Goals. This is the first step for defining a plan or strategy for your team. Goals are an essential part of developing and growing your leadership. Goals provide focus and direction for you and your team. Well-defined goals help you to identify what your desired outcomes and results will be.

The S.MA.R^2.T. or Specific, Measurable, Action-Oriented, Relevant/Realistic, and Time-Bound model is a structured tool that allows for a critical analysis of goals and how to achieve them.

- **SPECIFIC**: Specific means the goal needs to be as concrete as possible. Why do you want to achieve and accomplish the goal? Be as specific as possible to reduce ambiguity. One key way to reduce ambiguity and uncertainty is to have goals that are clear, focused, specific, and intentional. **Bottom Line:** When you set a specific goal, you know what actions you need to take to accomplish the goal and you realize which actions to take to fulfill your goals.

- **MEASURABLE:** A measurable goal is real, quantifiable, and feasible. It is difficult to arrive at your destination without knowing where you are going. A measurable goal lets you know clearly that you have arrived at your destination. **Bottom Line**: When you quantify your goal, you can measure your progress. You can actually achieve it within your measurable criteria.

- **ACTION-ORIENTED:** Action-oriented goals mean that you will accomplish an activity that produces outcomes and results. It is essential that before you start working on your goals, you must make sure that those goals are actionable and that you can take action to achieve them. A goal without action is a dream unrealized. **Bottom Line**: An action-oriented goal is a realistic goal that can be accomplished in a short time. Your goals should drive you to take all necessary actions to achieve the desired goals.

- **RELEVANT AND REALISTIC**: Relevant and Realistic goals are challenging but achievable and motivate you because they are important to you. Your goals should be relevant enough to be life changing. **Bottom Line:** Relevant and realistic goals should inspire you enough to change to achieve the goal. An effective goal can also provide you with great motivation to take consistent action to achieve your goals.

- **TIME-BOUND:** Time-bound means there is a definable and a finite period for completion. Example: In order to be eligible for the supervisory position, I will attend three leadership seminars on March 22, June 15, and October 5. **Bottom Line:** Your goal should have a deadline. You do not want goals that drag on forever. You will achieve nothing with open-ended goals. Time-bound your goals or you will never accomplish them.

DETERMINE YOUR PRIORITIES: In order to have clarity of purpose you need to focus on and prioritize a small number of key goals. Your decision and actions will reflect your leadership priorities.

You can choose to focus on all of these competing issues and matters, or you can choose to focus your mind on things that truly matter and are important to your Unstoppable Leadership.

If you focus on too many goals you could become overwhelmed at the thought of meeting them all, or you may feel like a failure for not accomplishing everything. By stating a specific goal, you can manage your time better and you can set your priorities more clearly.

The prioritized goals must align with your vision, mission, and strategy. When you narrow your focus and scope of your goals, the greater the chance you have of achieving them with positive outcomes.

When you finally have established the priorities of the goals, they must be clearly communicated to everyone in the organization. Managing your time will be easier if your priorities and goals are concrete, realistic, and communicated to those around you. As you begin to think about your goals, consider dividing them into long-term goals and short-term goals.

- Long-Term Goal (6+ Years)
- Long-Term Goal (4 Years)
- Mid-Term Goal (2 Years)
- Short-Term Goal (12 Months to 2 years)
- Short-Term Goal (6 to 12 months)
- Near-Term Goal (1 Week to 6 months)

DEFINE YOUR OBJECTIVES: Each day you create the future with your focus, clarity, and intentional actions. Goals are the starting point for developing your leadership strategy. Objectives are the basis for achieving your goals. They are the inchstones to milestones needed to achieve your overall strategic plan.

Each goal should have a detailed objective that produces the desired outcome and produces positive goal achievement. People who understand the vision and mission of the leader can align their goals and values to the goals and values of the organization.

DESCRIBE YOUR TACTICS: Tactics are the operational steps necessary to meet the objectives. During this step, the participants are engaged in tactical thinking. The affective skill aligned with this step is tolerance for risk taking. As an intentional and Unstoppable Leader you are focused on where you want to go, you take the time to clarify, plan, chart out your journey, and you intentionally choose the parameters of your leadership.

DETAIL YOUR ACTION PLAN: Proper action planning is needed for goal-setting, otherwise you will lose your focus and get derailed. The final step of goal setting is writing it down in an executable plan of action. An actionable plan creates a clear and intentional strategy for you to achieve your goals. You are moving ideas from mere thought to actionable solutions.

SUMMARY

Unstoppable Leaders do not lead because of power, position, or permission, they lead because they have the courage to lead and courage to take action. To achieve great things as an Unstoppable Leader, you have to take a risk and lead others.

THE FIRST PRINCIPLES

You need the resolute courage to lead with your inspiring vision and forge ahead each day despite criticism and the naysayers. You must have the courage to believe in your abilities, capabilities, and skills to lead in a complex and chaotic world. An Unstoppable Leader has the courage to live greatly and see opportunity in adversity.

CHARACTER CHECK

1. How courageous are you as a leader?

2. Do you stand up for what is right?

3. Do you stand up for your team?

4. Do you stand by your decisions?

LOOKING INTO THE MIRROR

After reading this chapter, review and reflect on the ideas and concepts presented. Think about what opportunities, challenges, resources, or blind spots you may encounter when you begin your growth and development journey.

Use the following questions to help you grow and develop.

1. How will I incorporate this principle into my leadership development?

2. What opportunity and resources exist for me to use this principle this week, this year?

3. What blind spots may derail me from using this principle?

THE FIRST PRINCIPLES

COMMITMENT TIME

- ✓ Courage is a key factor in developing and maintaining a courageous mindset

- ✓ Real courage is facing an overwhelming trial without fear of failure and picking yourself up when you stumble

- ✓ Lead with courage and with principles

- ✓ Each day you need the courage to challenge your comfort zones and face your fears

- ✓ Courage is making the tough choices in the face of hardship

- ✓ Courage defines your success as a leader

- ✓ Courage is transformational

- ✓ Confidence is your greatest personal resource and resilience factor

- ✓ Lead with boldness and audacity

- ✓ Each act of leadership courage builds your self-confidence as a leader

- ✓ Confidence is your greatest personal resource and resilience factor

THE FIRST PRINCIPLES

LEADERSHIP NOTES

CHAPTER FIVE

THE FOCUS PRINCIPLE

LEADING WITH A POSITIVE AND OPTIMISTIC OUTLOOK

"Our greatest freedom is the freedom to choose our attitude."
Viktor E. Frankl

On February 18, 2009, CMSgt Todd Small and I traveled to Thule, Greenland, to see and talk to our Airmen stationed at Thule Air Base. Thule AB is 750 miles north of the Arctic Circle, approximately 550 miles east of the North Magnetic Pole, and is locked in by ice nine months out of the year.

Why did we go in the dead of winter? The 821st Airmen operated nine months out of the year in extreme cold, little to no sunlight from November to January, and during the winter they experience storms that are a deadly combination of wind, snow, and sub-zero temperatures. In order to let them know we cared and to experience how our Airmen lived throughout their assignment, we needed to experience the winter.

As a leader, you need to go where your people live and see how they operate on a day-to-day basis. By going during the cold and dark winter, we showed, by our actions, that we cared about them enough to experience what they experience. Additionally, arriving in the wintertime increased the trust and credibility factor for our visit.

When we arrived at Thule AB it was -35°, the air was piercingly cold, and it penetrated right through your clothing. As we stepped off the plane, the first breath burned nose and lungs. It was **COLD!**

After a few hours of rest and a quick breakfast, we headed out to see the Airmen at their work centers. At Thule, the work centers are not clustered together, they are spread out all over the icy landmass that required us to travel along frozen and iced over roads to see every Airman. Spread out along the route, for safety reasons, are emergency storm shelters that provide a safe haven during a sudden winter storm.

Chief Small and I visited every work center at Thule, AB, and presented our coins to the Thule Top Performers. We were met by upbeat and positive Airmen in each work center we visited. We experienced positive attitudes at each work center throughout the day.

Visiting work centers was one of the highlights of our trip and I needed to find out the secret to their positive outlook on life. Before we left Thule AB, we had an opportunity to hold a Leadership Call to pass on information and answer any questions the Airmen had for us.

During the Leadership Call, I finally asked what the secret ingredient was to why everyone was positive and optimistic throughout the day. A young Airman stood up and answered the question.

> It is by choice. We choose to be positive and optimistic while we are here. When we arrive and attend our 'Welcome to Thule AB briefing' we are briefed on Thule Survival skills. How to survive while driving in a winter storm, how to prevent frostbite, and how to live in 24-hour darkness. Then we have a brief on resiliency and remaining positive during our assignment.
>
> It is all a matter of outlook and choice. I can choose to be miserable and hate the assignment or I can choose to look at the positive aspects of the assignment and get to know new people and have new opportunities.
>
> Our attitude influences everything we do here while stationed at Thule and in the rest of our careers. Our attitudes are a reflection of our feelings, moods, and beliefs. My attitude will determine how I will perceive and react to my day. I choose to be positive and optimistic.

LEADERSHIP MINDSET

Attitude is infectious! How often have you asked someone what kind of mood did the boss arrive in this morning? If he/she arrived with a good attitude, it was going to be a good day. If he/she arrived with a bad attitude, it was going to be a bad day for everyone.

As a leader, your attitude is important. It influences how your day turns out and it influences how well your team will perform. Attitude is your state of mind toward others or situations. It is an outward expression of how you are feeling or reacting inside. It shows in how you talk, act, react, and in your facial and body expressions.

Your team can tell almost immediately what kind of attitude you came to work with by your behavior. Your attitude is how you, as the leader, interact with your team, your organization, and if applicable, your customers.

HOW WILL I LEAD TODAY?

Each morning ask yourself--What will my attitude be today? Your leadership attitude affects everybody who encounters you and affects work productivity, innovation, and collaboration. Your attitude is the alpha and omega of your leadership. How you choose to react and act each day starts with your attitude.

Attitude is an indispensable part of an Unstoppable Leader and Unstoppable Leadership. A bad leadership attitude can infect a team and an organization just like a computer worm infects a computer and a network. A negative attitude can spread negativity throughout the team and organization, sour working relationships, and affect overall team productivity.

However, a positive and encouraging attitude can encourage, inspire, and rejuvenate an entire organization to greater heights. Attitude is your state of mind toward others or situations. It is an outward expression of how you are feeling or reacting inside.

POSITIVE ATTITUDE

The true power of a positive attitude is more than positive thinking; it is a way of life. One of your first choices as a leader is to establish and maintain a positive attitude. A positive attitude is a powerful leadership mindset and leadership tool.

Your leadership attitude has the potential to encourage or discourage. As a leader, your optimism affects your team, your organization, and your bottom line. It is a continuous state of mind and leadership focus. It is a mindset that no matter what leadership challenges you face, you keep your life and your leadership attitude focused on the positive aspects.

You need to believe that life is about positive opportunities and possibilities and be optimistic about who and what you can become. You will handle life differently if you shape your focus toward the positive versus allowing yourself to focus on the negative. A positive outlook will tell you that there is a light at the end of every tunnel.

The amazing thing about a leadership attitude is that you have the ability to control and manage your attitude. Emotions, moods, and leadership attitude are key reasons why I think emotional intelligence is an important leadership principle.

EMOTIONAL STATES AND THE LEADER

Each leader is susceptible to his or her emotional state and moods at work. Understanding how to manage the emotions and moods can make you a better leader. According to Daniel Goleman in his book *Emotional Intelligence*, self-awareness, self-management, social awareness, and relationship management are vital assets for a leader. An emotionally intelligent leader is aware of how their attitude affects others.

Emotional intelligence is the ability to understand that it is not what happens to you that determines your attitude, but how you decide to respond. Emotional intelligence is a key part of your attitude. Emotional intelligence helps you keep your mind focused by keeping your emotional state in check.

To have a great attitude in leadership, you must be constantly aware of the things that are influencing you and then you need to make a choice on how to react.

To be a great leader you need to understand empathy. Empathy is the understanding of others by being aware of their needs, perspectives, feelings, and concerns, and sensing the developmental needs of others.

Stress, emotions, and moods are key reasons why emotional intelligence is part of a disciplined mind. You are susceptible to your emotional state and moods in life. Understanding how to manage your emotions and moods can make you a better person.

OPTIMISTIC OUTLOOK

Optimism is looking at life and expecting the best outcome to happen no matter what circumstances life hands you. Optimism begins in your mind and changes your attitude toward life. Being optimistic is being positive and being your own agent of hope. Hope gives you the determination and willpower to overcome challenges.

A negative outlook would convince you that the light at the end of the tunnel is a train heading your way. By focusing on the positives in your life, you create an optimistic outlook in your life and begin to see a life full of possibilities.

Looking at leadership in an optimistic way provides you the confidence and courage to tackle challenges and issues head on. Being optimistic means you are not afraid to seek out leadership opportunities.

You see the positive aspects of leadership versus the negative. With confidence, you can face life's challenges head on and know that you will survive and thrive. Confidence is indispensable to an Unstoppable Leader. Confidence is an ardent belief in yourself, your capabilities, and your ability.

A confident attitude is your greatest personal resource and leadership resilience factor. It is a life changer. You control your confidence level. Confidence is the inner voice that steels you and lets you know you have the capability and the ability to achieve your dreams and goals.

FOCUS AND INTENTIONALITY

Why are focus, clarity, and intentionality important? Because what you focus on intentionally will shape your team and organization. As an Unstoppable Leader, you need to have focus, clarity, and intentionality in your leadership.

Focus, clarity, and intentionality are Unstoppable Leadership requirements. Focus, clarity, and intentionality are the concentrating actions of determining your future outcomes today. The world today remains complex, uncertain, and ever-changing.

Each day your mind races with your own thoughts, ideas, and intentions while being bombarded with the noise and clutter of the day-to-day issues of work, home, and life. Collectively, these things compete for your attention and can cause you to become unfocused and distracted.

Clarity and focus helps a leader reduce the ambiguity and uncertainty of leadership. Clarity and focus gives you the leadership capability to make decisions quickly. It is important because where you put your focus on intentionally, your life and leadership will follow.

FOCUSED AND DISCIPLINED

One way we develop young men and women to prepare for the combat environment is by developing and readying their bodies and their minds for uncertainty, complexity, and ambiguity. We concentrate on developing a focused and disciplined mind.

Having a focused and disciplined mind is a mindset of understanding the world with clarity and focus and creating the mental toughness you need to operate and function in chaos and crisis. A focused and disciplined mind is dedicated to preparing and understanding the uncertainty and complexity of your leadership environment.

Developing a focused and intentional mind is a way of thinking with clarity despite uncertainty and simplifying the complex while under pressure. It is intentionally thinking of possibilities and opportunities. Your day-to-day focus will shape your leadership focus. You understand and can operate in a volatile, uncertain, complex, and ambiguous world with focus, clarity, and intentionality.

THE 8P FOCUS

In the book, *You Are Unstoppable!*, I introduced the 6P Focus as a deliberate and intentional tool to help you to have focus and clarity in your life. In this book we expand upon the 6P model and introduce the 8P model as a deliberate and intentional tool to help you with focus and clarity as a leader.

The 8Ps are--planning, preparation, priorities, people, passion, performance, persistence, and perseverance. The 8Ps add priorities and people to the model as two areas a leader must intentionally focus on each day.

Priorities allow a leader to focus on what truly is important to accomplish and where to expend energy and resources. People-focused leadership is important for a leader since leadership is all about inspiring and motivating people to accomplish the desired mission.

At the very beginning of your leadership journey you need to plan and prepare for your challenges and crucibles. The 8P Focus is about choosing where to put your time, passion, and attention and balancing your leadership priorities.

The 8P Focus is a deliberate tool you can use to see the big picture to plan and prepare, make effective decisions, and set and establish team and organizational goals. It helps you lead with focus, clarity, and intentionality. By choosing to lead with focus and intentionality you begin to see through the daily uncertainty and ambiguity.

Leadership focus and intentionality has a compound effect on your leadership capability. When you are focused and intentional with your choices and decisions, you have clarity in your leadership and professional life. You lead by design instead of by default. Leading with clarity, focus, and intentionality allows you to set clear and actionable goals.

The 8P Focus is important because as a leader of a team or an organization you need to know where you want to go, establish goals, set priorities, and then lead.

PLANNING: All successful leadership begins with the planning step. Planning is the process of developing actions and plans to attain your desired goals or outcomes. When making your plans and subsequent actions, consider what you truly want to accomplish and what effects are needed to achieve your outcome.

Strategic planning is important in project and program management to reduce uncertainty and ambiguity; it is vitally important in leadership. Planning also helps reduce anxiety and increases the probability that you will achieve the goals that you have established.

To shape your leadership you must know what you want to accomplish with your team and your organization. Why do you need to effectively plan? You need to plan and lay the groundwork to effectively guide your team and organization to success.

Planning allows you to establish a map of success, chart the course, and establish goals and objectives to achieve your organizational mission. Therefore, the very first step to being a successful leader is to take time to plan and organize what you want to accomplish. Planning provides you the ***WHAT*** you need to do.

PREPARATION: The second step is to prepare yourself, your team, or organization to achieve the goals and objectives. Being an Unstoppable Leader means intentionally leading with focus and clarity each day.

Preparation is the key to successful leadership and is the trademark of successful leaders worldwide. The more time you prepare yourself, the better equipped you are for the leadership challenges and crucibles.

Preparation is the process of equipping and focusing yourself on achieving your plan. You must have the right mindset and focus to carry out your plan successfully. Roman philosopher Seneca said, "Luck is what happens when preparation meets opportunity." Make yourself lucky by being prepared. How well are you prepared as a leader? How well have you prepared your team or organization?

By properly preparing you can take advantage of leadership opportunities and possibilities and leverage them to your benefit. By effectively preparing your team you provide them the opportunity to overcome inertia and adapt when challenged. Preparation gives you an opportunistic focus and clarity. There is no such idea of being over prepared, but there are consequences of being under prepared.

PRIORITIES: An essential tool for clarity and focus in leading yourself and your team is priorities. If planning and preparation establish the roadmap of goals and objectives for your life and leadership, then priorities establish the order and importance of goal achievement.

Setting priorities forces you to intentionally think about what is most important and where you need to focus as a leader first. As a leader of a team or organization you need to set priorities to accomplish the goals that are most important. Priorities provide you the clarity of purpose to where you need to expend precious resources to achieve the desired goals. Priorities provide you the **WHY** you need to do these first and establish the starting line.

PEOPLE: People-focused leadership involves setting and clarifying organizational and developmental leadership expectations. Letting your people know what you and the organization expects of them in the area of growth and development is important.

Your people need to own their leadership development and understand their importance in the organization and how you plan to invest in them. This information will communicate trust, develop responsibility, and reinforce the importance of growth and development to the organization.

With the globalization of the world economies, the rate and pace of change, new emerging technologies, and the chaotic nature of the world today, organizations are reliant on knowledge-enabled, globally connected, and highly competent employees to remain competitive.

Therefore, it is an organizational imperative you invest in developing your people systematically and persistently. Developing leaders in a deliberate process guarantees you will produce the requisite leadership for the future.

By growing and developing your people you are building a leadership bench for your team and your organization. This is an organizational imperative and a necessity. These are the principles of continuous development, continuous coaching, and continuously encouraging your people.

PASSION: Leadership is not necessarily associated with rank and position, but is fundamentally associated with qualities such as drive, vision, innovation, creativity, and passion. This step is a critical leadership talent. You must have passion to achieve greatly in your personal and professional life. How passionate are you as a leader? Do you show passion each day as you lead?

Passion is the spark that ignites you each day to lead your team and organization. It is the energy of an inspired life and Unstoppable Leadership. Being the best in your life, career, or leadership requires purposeful passion. Passion is the lynchpin of great leadership.

A leader must be passionate about people and want to develop and grow them. Unstoppable Leadership comes from within and is fueled by the passion and desire to change, improve, and inspire people each day.

PERFORMANCE: The next step is performance. How do you perform daily as a leader? Do you make the right decision? Do you take appropriate actions? How well is your team performing? You need to take action and perform to your utmost each day to lead with unstoppable first principles.

Your success as a leader and the success of your team or organization should not be by accident but by your designed performance. You must strive each day to be intentional in your personal and professional life. You need to passionately pursue your purpose in life and relentlessly challenge yourself to become a better leader each day.

PERSISTENCE: Persistence is leadership in action. Persistence allows you to keep working toward established goals or objectives until you reach the desired outcome. It is pressing on toward the goal despite all odds. The overall objective of persistence is to achieve goals or outcomes in yourself as a leader.

Perhaps the greatest display of leadership is persisting when the going gets tough. Persistence is the great measure of your character. Your persistence is, in fact, the true measure of your belief in yourself and your ability to succeed. Each time you persist in the face of adversity and disappointment you build the habit of persistence.

By persisting you become a more disciplined and focused leader. You develop as an Unstoppable Leader with the iron quality of determination and success.

Persistence is a key step and an indispensable leadership attribute. You must constantly press forward as a leader no matter the challenge, no matter the struggle. How persistent are you as a leader to lead your team through challenges? How persistent is your team to achieve goals? How persistent is your organization toward achieving success?

You must stand in the face of leadership adversity and choose to weather the storm. Persistence is your willingness to keep yourself and your team focused on the task and keep moving toward mission completion.

PERSEVERANCE: All great leaders have had to endure tremendous trials and tribulations before reaching the heights of leadership success and achievement. The strength of their character was manifested in their unshakable resolve, focus, and intentionality.

Perseverance requires your entire emotional, physical, and spiritual forte to tolerate or overcome the situation. By persevering and not giving in, you gain strength in your life and leadership.

Leadership perseverance is the ability and capability to endure difficult situations and challenges with resolute determination and to stay in a situation even when you would rather give up. You must never quit on yourself, your team, or your organization. You must never give in on achieving your dreams. How well do you and your team persevere when pressed to reach goals in a short time? How well does your organization persevere during tough economic times?

When you persevere as a leader, you are telling your team, your organization, and the world that you are in it to win it. Perseverance is the power to survive and thrive.

Perseverance will carry you forward and over any obstacle you may encounter. You build pride, power, and self-esteem into your character and your personality and become stronger and more resolute as a leader.

THE 8PS AND THE 4 STARS

During my career, I had the honor and privilege to be the Command Senior Enlisted Leader for four great leaders; two were 4-Star Generals and two became 4-Star Generals. Each of them displayed certain characteristics of the 8P Focus.

General C. Robert Kehler
Preparation and Planning

General Kehler's focus was on planning and preparation and his strengths were foresight and global awareness. I first met General Kehler when he assumed command of Air Force Space Command in October 2007. At the time, I was serving as the 14th Air Force and Joint Functional Component Command for Space Command Chief.

During his briefing to the Commanders and Senior Enlisted Leaders, he detailed his concern about the uncertainty and complexity of today's battle space and the future challenges for the Space environment. He challenged the Commanders and Senior Enlisted to begin thinking, planning, and preparing how the command could meet the uncertainties of a challenging future.

In January 2011, General Kehler assumed command of USSTRATCOM where I had the opportunity to be his Command Senior Enlisted Leader. As he did at Air Force Space Command, he held a briefing for the Commanders and Senior Enlisted Leaders after he assumed command. One of his key focus areas, and eventually a command priority, was to prepare for the uncertainty and complexity of the national security landscape. He challenged those present to think how USSTRATCOM and its Unified Command Plan missions would operate in an environment of persistent conflict, complexity, and uncertainty that stretched across all warfighting domains of air, sea, land, space, and cyberspace.

General Kehler's focus was on planning and preparing the Command by developing our people, processes, and programs to meet unexpected challenges of the future. We needed to be flexible, adaptive, and collaborative in our thinking and operations to deal with surprise and to meet the uncertainties of tomorrow's unforeseen problems.

General Kevin P. Chilton
Priorities and People

General Chilton's focus was on mission-priority and people and his strengths were alliance and relationship building, character authenticity, and critical thinking. General Chilton's leadership strategy was through mission prioritization. His focus was on prioritization of USSTRATCOM Unified Command Plan missions to ensure every person assigned knew their importance and priority. He established his mission priorities based on the importance of the assigned mission to National Security.

Throughout his time as the commander he would state, "If everything is important, then nothing is important." By setting priorities for the command, everyone knew what was important and the order of precedence. When briefing others about his priorities, he would talk about how in his role as the Commander of USSTRATCOM he had to juggle several missions daily, but only one mission, the nuclear mission, would have grave damage upon the National Security of the Nation. The nuclear mission was the #1 priority for USSTRATCOM.

Another key priority for General Chilton was people. General Chilton was an "enlisted persons general". From January through December of 2009, United States Strategic Command celebrated the "Year of the Enlisted Global Warfighter" and the "Global Warrior" enlisted force development program to focus on the history, heritage, and mission of Strategic Air Command and United States Strategic Command and the contributions of the enlisted force in its missions. It was an important initiative for recognizing the enlisted force and the contributions they provided United States Strategic Command.

In his letter recognizing the year, he stated: "Every enlisted Soldier, Sailor, Marine, and Airman is critical to mission success. It is imperative that our enlisted warriors continue to be the capable, credible, and faithful men and women America has come to expect. I expect leaders at all levels to embrace these two programs and encourage participation by the enlisted personnel in your work areas."

General Carlton "Dewey" Everhart
Passion and Performance

General Everhart was a leader full of passion for life and people and his strengths were inspiration, encouragement, and developing leaders.

I had the opportunity to work for, then Colonel Everhart, at Altus Air Force Base when he assumed command in September of 2005. Under his leadership, two unique talent development programs--Airmen's Time and Enlisted Force Development--were highly successful and were emulated by the Air Force.

Airmen's Time produced a new focus on total force professional and leadership development of the officer and civilian work force resulting in a consolidated Warrior Professional Development Center. The leadership philosophy change produced outcomes that validated the Airmen's Time development process. It changed from an individual leadership development focus to a collective leadership development focus.

In the end, Airmen's Time: The Altus Concept was a highly successful journey. It developed a strong organizational culture based on core values, teamwork, diversity, respect, leadership development, and transformational change.

It built a culture of innovation, teamwork, and growth that spread throughout the wing and developed leaders for the future. It developed a strong outcomes-focused performance culture within all organizations and fostered a leadership culture that crossed group boundaries and established a strong team culture.

General William Shelton
Persistence and Perseverance

General Shelton was a leader of persistence and perseverance and his strengths were focused purpose and strategic vision. General Shelton hired me as the 14th Air Force Command Chief as I was returning to the United States from my year assignment to the Middle East.

I had the unique opportunity to see his vision become a reality as he built the Joint Space Operations Center (JSPOC) into a consolidated operational space command and control and space situational awareness center.

I arrived after the JSPOC had relocated to a new facility, but just in time for the move of the 1st Space Control Squadron and Unified Space Vault from Cheyenne Mountain to the JSPOC. As General Shelton's vison took shape, it provided an integrated space capability for the Nation and the Warfighter.

Despite some obstacles, he championed the strengths of the net-centric and space tracking capabilities of the JSPOC to operate in the space domain. Under his leadership, dogged determination, and drive, he built a first-rate space operations center that is vital to understanding the space environment, critical to the warfighter, and is a National asset.

SUMMARY

Leadership is demanding, so you must prepare yourself mentally, physically, spiritually, and emotionally to be an Unstoppable Leader.

To lead with focus, clarity, and intentionality means you need to remove ambiguity and uncertainty by establishing clear goals, clear objectives, a clear strategy, and clear tactics. Clarity and focus provides you the decision-making ability to make critical and timely decisions in times of chaos and crisis.

CHARACTER CHECK

1. What is your attitude as a leader?
2. What is your leadership presence each day?
3. Are you optimistic and positive?
4. Do you encourage and inspire?
5. Are you an Agent of Hope?

LOOKING INTO THE MIRROR

After reading this chapter, review and reflect on the ideas and concepts presented. Think about what opportunities, challenges, resources, or blind spots you may encounter when you begin your growth and development journey.

Use the following questions to help you grow and develop.

1. How will I incorporate this principle into my leadership development?
2. What opportunity and resources exist for me to use this principle this week, this year?
3. What blind spots may derail me from using this principle?

THE FIRST PRINCIPLES

COMMITMENT TIME

- ✓ Passion fuels the spark that energizes a team to achieve greatness

- ✓ Persistence is the power to achieve success, no matter the circumstance

- ✓ Seek to achieve mastery of your life and leadership to lead greatly

- ✓ Perseverance is the cornerstone of Unstoppable Leadership

- ✓ Persistence permits you to attain victory as a leader when others have long abandoned the journey

- ✓ Leadership resiliency is vital in the performance of a leader

- ✓ Each day you lead is an opportunity to be intentional and focused

- ✓ By choosing to lead with focus, you begin to see the simple answer to complex issues

- ✓ An optimistic leadership outlook creates an optimistic team mindset

- ✓ Lead each day with a positive and optimistic attitude

LEADERSHIP NOTES

CHAPTER SIX

THE ADAPTABILITY PRINCIPLE

Learning to be Flexible, Adaptive, and Resilient in Your Leadership Challenges

"Fortify thyself with contentment: that is an impregnable stronghold."
Epiticus

The Colonel stood on the small hill peering into the smoke filled valley below. Silently he assessed the chaos that surrounded him--the smell of fear, the stench of week old sweat and blood, and the overpowering scent of acrid gun smoke filled his senses.

He looked around and saw his men, their faces black with burning powder, and he knew the gravity of the situation. He and his men were in trouble. They were almost out of ammo and the enemy was readying themselves for a final attack. He needed a victory if he wanted to live to see the sun another day.

Colonel Chamberlain could see the multiple outcomes of the battle playing out in his mind if he did not act. He did not want to die on the hill. Colonel Chamberlain needed to be flexible and adaptive and create the battlefield effect in order to achieve his desired outcome.

He was determined that he and his men would live another day. His mind raced over the day's events as the outcome to the problem slowly filled his mind. He rallied his officers and informed them what he planned to do. For Chamberlain there was only one thing left-- sweep down the hill in a bold counterattack.

Colonel Joshua Chamberlain gave the order, 'Fix bayonets!' to the men on Little Round Top and the men readied themselves for the next onslaught. Colonel Chamberlain and his men charged forward and swung his line down the hill in a right wheel forward movement that concentrated his forces down onto the charging Confederates like a scythe reaping wheat. The Confederates, stunned at the audacity of the counterattack, dropped their rifles, retreated, and then surrendered. Joshua Chamberlain achieved victory that day and lived another day.

Throughout his life, Joshua Chamberlain, the college professor-turned-soldier, was a good example of an Unstoppable Leader. He served in 20 battles, was cited for valor and gallantry four times, had six horses shot from under him, was wounded six times in battle, and achieved the rank of Brigadier General.

Because of the authentic character and leadership of Joshua Chamberlain, General U.S. Grant selected him to receive the formal surrender of Robert E. Lee's army at Appomattox Court House in April 1865.

After the war, Joshua Chamberlain served four terms as Governor of Maine and then went on to serve as the President of Bowdoin College. He taught every subject at Bowdoin with the exception of science and mathematics, and was fluent in nine languages.

As a final act of gratitude, Congress bestowed on him the Medal of Honor in 1893. Joshua Chamberlain was a disciplined learner but a flexible and adaptive leader.

He focused on continuous learning throughout his life, he sought out mentors to help him be a better soldier, and he used those abilities and capabilities to win and survive life's battles.

NO ROOM FOR BYSTANDERS

From August 2006 to July 2007, I deployed as the Command Senior Enlisted Leader to the 386th Air Expeditionary Wing in support of Operation Iraqi Freedom. Over the course of the year and three Air and Space Expeditionary Force rotations I had the leadership opportunity to lead and take care of 11,000 Airmen.

The combat airlift wing consisted of five groups in 11 different locations and conducted eight unique missions that covered an area of 25,000 square miles.

The disparate missions ranged from Base Operations, Logistics, and Medical to Combat Airlift, Convoy Operations, and Detainee Operations.

During my yearlong deployment, I took a leadership-by-example and a front-line approach to leading the Airmen. I went where they went, I traveled the roads they traveled, and I conducted the missions they conducted.

Missions included flight line aircraft maintenance at midnight, combat airlift, outside the wire ground operations, and detainee operations missions, along with carving and serving turkey during Thanksgiving. If my people were there, I was there.

However, the one mission that left a lasting leadership effect on me was Area Surveillance Operations (ASO) in Safwan and Um Qasr, Iraq. ASO was a vehicle and foot patrol operation to look for improvised explosive devices commonly known as IEDs, standoff enemy threat positions, and insurgent operations activities.

The mission was to dominate the battle space surrounding Forward Operating Base Bucca. This was done through integrated base defense and by aggressively securing multiple convoy routes utilizing mounted and dismounted combat patrols within a 300 square kilometer Area of Influence. **Bottom Line: Keep the roads clear so the convoys got through and people didn't die.**

THE FIRST PRINCIPLES

The battle space the Airmen and Soldiers operated in had 40 IED attacks on previous patrols resulting in the loss of lives, to include the death of the first female Security Forces Airman, Senior Airman Elizabeth Nicole Jacobsen. Over the course of my deployed time, I conducted multiple mounted combat patrols and dismounted combat patrols with Airmen and Soldiers.

There are two modes of travel to Bucca--by air on Blackhawk helicopters or by land via Army combat convoy. Both are dangerous transportation methods. Throughout the year, I convoyed countless times on cross-border convoys through the dangerous highways and roads of Southern Iraq. From my first crossing to my last, the pucker factor remained the same.

However, no matter if I headed out to Bucca with Soldiers via an Army combat convoy or out with our Airmen to conduct mounted or dismounted combat patrols, the Troop Commander briefed me on why we were there, what his expectations were, what my role was to be, and what my responsibilities were during the convoy or patrol.

The most important and most critical part of the briefing was "there are no passengers or bystanders on a combat convoy or combat patrol. You are a combat-trained warrior ready to engage and suppress the enemy if so challenged. Your actions will determine if you live or die today."

The troop commander's "in your face" reminder was a wakeup call to everyone heading out on that day.

You must stay focused on the mission situations, have clarity of mind, and be intentional with your actions or they could be your last. **Bottom Line: There are no second chances in combat.**

NOT A SPECTATOR SPORT

"Life is not a spectator sport…if you're going to spend your whole life in the grandstand just watching what goes on, in my opinion you're wasting your life."
Jackie Robinson

Jackie Robinson was right. Life and Leadership are not spectator sports and today, there is no room for leaders who want to be passengers or bystanders in leadership. Your actions will determine if people will follow your lead or find a new leader.

The reality is that the world changed and the expectation for leaders has changed. The world is a volatile, uncertain, complex, and ambiguous environment (VUCA). For a leader, this means you must be able to operate in a dynamic, complex, uncertain, and unclear environment. To make it clear as the Troop Commander did for me, VUCA means:

Volatile: The speed, size, and scale of change in the world today has a great impact on events around the globe almost instantaneously. Change is a constant in a VUCA environment, and to remain successful and unstoppable you must be able to positively respond to continuous change.

You must learn to have the capability to lead through continuous change and learn to be adaptive and flexible throughout the change process. An example is that people are no longer limited to Ocean boundaries or imaginary lines drawn on a map to connect with other people. They reach out daily via the internet and social media to build a virtual nation.

Uncertainty: World events are unpredictable and this unpredictability makes it impossible to prepare for the unknown and uncertainty.

In a VUCA environment, improvising is being able to create opportunities and solutions in an unexpected challenge or situation. You must be flexible and adaptive to the situation and prepare to handle challenges.

Complexity: The nature of the world combined with the volatility and uncertainty of global events creates an environment of confusion and difficulty for today's leaders. It is chaotic and unpredictable. A leader today needs to understand market globalization, global migrations, global influences, social media, technological advances, and the unyielding pace of change.

Ambiguity: Today, there is a lack of clarity or transparency surrounding world events. It is hard to predict what threats are in the world if you do not know the who, what, or why things are happening. A VUCA environment requires your full focus on the situation; it requires that you have clarity of mind and purpose and intentional leadership action. It requires 100% of your leadership capability to lead in the world today.

To lead effectively you need to be flexible, adaptive, and resilient and learn to incorporate the following adaptive concepts into your leadership:

- Develop flexible and adaptive thinking strategies through linear and non-linear thinking

- Learn how to look at the world holistically and strategically

- Become globally interconnected through social interactions

- Be a lifelong learner and learn new skills and talents to help you lead in the new normal

- Learn to communicate cross-functionally and multi-culturally

- Learn to make decisions at the pace of change

- Engage in "out-of-the-box" and synchronicity thinking

- Read and stay current on global trends and changes

GLOBAL IMPACT OF LEADERSHIP

The overarching theme in the collected data in both the military and in the corporate world is a call to develop and prepare leaders to operate in a world of globalization, global diasporas, global markets, social media, technological advances, and the unyielding pace of change in both the military and business operations.

This multidimensional leadership chaos and organizational complexity creates challenges for today's leaders to lead effectively.

Pace of Change: Leaders must be flexible, adaptive, and pioneering. They must be able to improvise, adapt, create, and disruptively innovate as rapidly as the current pace of change. A leader must be able to effectively lead and manage change to adapt and adjust to a dynamic and ever-changing global market.

Virtual Markets and Social Media: A leader must be able to move and operate in the virtual marketplace and the social media domain. A leader must understand how to reach out via the internet, social media, technologically, and through search engines to communicate and connect with people around the world.

Global Transformation: A leader must have a clear understanding how technology, diversity, the redistribution of people on earth, failing nation-states, and the interactions among diverse cultural groups affect organizations in a global market and global society.

Globally Aware: A leader must be multiculturally astute and understand how to work with peoples of different countries, cultures, religions, and worldviews. A leader needs to be culturally smart and talented to use this cultural awareness to lead across barriers and generations and understand how to work with people of different countries and cultures.

A leader needs to lead across multicultural and national boundaries to increase the effectiveness of the organization. Relationship building results in both personal and professional development.

GLOBAL LEADERSHIP COMPETENCIES

Risk-Taker: A leader must be able to demonstrate the capability to act in an influential, urgent, and steadfast way to realize outcomes and results. They do not fear risk but comprehend and manage it to achieve desired results. A leader encourages and rewards creativity, innovation, and continuous improvement.

Divergent and Convergent Thinker: A leader needs to engage in "out-of-the-box" synchronicity thinking and think at the tactical, operational, and strategic level when looking at ambiguous and complex problems to develop innovative strategies and tactics.

Foresight: A leader needs to be able to think short-term and long-term with a future-orientation focus. They must be able to see the "Big Picture" and have a mental picture of what the organization should look like and be in the future and provide an inspiring and achievable vision.

Team and Organization Designer: A leader must be a master at networking, relationships, and alliance building. They must understand that the relationship of the leader and their team is built on trust. A leader must be able to enlarge and empower all team members to work together and across functional areas.

Entrepreneur and Intrapreneur Mindset: This concept builds on the Unstoppable Leadership model. The model is an Inside out/Outside leadership model focused on developing yourself first before you can lead others effectively. The Entrepreneur Mindset is about innovation, risk taking, effects and outcomes focus, and influential impact.

The Intrapreneur Mindset is about adding value within the organization by leading with the core values, leading authentically, and leading intentionally. Both mindsets are needed to be an Unstoppable Leader. You need to be able to positively influence the moral element of an organization and determine the outcome of situations.

You must remain focused on the organizational goals and leverage all available resources to achieve that goal.

A leader needs to be able to critically analyze problems and situations and foresee the second, third, and fourth order of effects of proposed policies or actions. Additionally, a leader needs to think long-term, be future-oriented, and have a mental picture of what the organization should look like and be in the future.

MEETING THE CHALLENGE

The mantle of leadership is not something you wear on the outside, it begins from within your character. Leadership is the life you live, it is not a part you play. The mantle of leadership is not easy, and in fact, at times it can feel like a yoke instead. Being a leader means you will face many challenges that are unpredictable, uncertain, ambiguous, and complex in nature.

Today, the speed and pace of change coupled with global interconnectedness of markets and people has transformed the leader's operational landscape. To succeed in a VUCA environment, an Unstoppable Leader must:

- Embrace Uncertainty
- Embrace Ambiguity
- Embrace Flexibility
- Embrace Complexity
- Embrace and Lead Change

We need leaders who can adapt to rapid changes, who can be flexible to deal with unpredictability and uncertainty, and who can be resilient to bounce back and deal with the same complex and ambiguous challenges the next day.

You must recognize that change is a constant and learn to be flexible, adaptive, and responsive to change. You need to be able to lead, communicate, and operate in the extant dynamic environment. You must be flexible and adaptive to quickly respond to crisis and change.

THE ART OF JUGGLING

If you are like me, life comes at you each day fast and furiously. Furthermore, if you are like me, you are juggling myriad of daily events and racing to the next to put out the next crisis without much planning or preparing for the new challenge.

This constant juggling act never allows time for reflection or review of your choices or decisions you made the day prior, let alone the last week. However, it is vitally, if not critically, important to frequently review and reflect on your major choices, chances, and changes in your life each day, month, and year.

You need to step back and assess your choices in order to see if you are wisely investing your time and energy in the things that are important to your future. Each day you have the opportunity to take action toward creating the life and future you want.

FLEXIBLE AND ADAPTIVE

A flexible and adaptive leader has a keen sense of the current global and organizational issues and the effects of an ever-changing and ambiguous world. Flexibility is the ability to adapt to new or different environments or situations. Flexibility is your ability to adapt with the changes in your life and leadership. Adaptability is your openness to change.

Throughout the chaos and uncertainty, you must maintain organizational effectiveness and personnel effectiveness during major changes in work tasks or work environment.

An Unstoppable Leader stops to assess the situations and asks the "what-ifs," then determines what effects are needed to create the desired outcome.

To succeed in this environment you must be more flexible, adaptive, and resilient. Being flexible, adaptive, and resilient is the ability to think on your feet and make choices in order to handle challenging situations, while at the same time being able to bounce back after the stress of the situation.

Flexible and adaptive leadership involves changing your behavior in appropriate ways as the situation changes. Flexibility is vital for you to overcome your daily life and leadership challenges. It gives you the ability to survive and succeed in leadership. You must be able to improvise, adapt, and overcome as rapidly as the current pace of change.

As a leader, flexibility means overcoming the challenge and completing the mission. You cannot control every aspect of your life; however, you can prepare yourself to be flexible and adaptive in how you react to unexpected life and leadership challenges.

Today's multidimensional leadership chaos and organizational complexity creates challenges for you to deal with and learn to lead through effectively. Being flexible is responding to changing or new situations in ways that move you forward.

WATER

A good example of being flexible and adaptive can be found in water. Water is an incredible unstoppable force of nature. At times, it can be dynamic, powerful, and resilient and other times, it can be still, motionless, and calming. Water is adaptive, ever-changing, and powerful. Water has unmatched metamorphosis properties and capabilities.

- Freeze it and it becomes ice
- Heat it and it becomes steam
- Pour it into a glass and it takes its shape
- Let it loose and it creates its own shape and path

As an Unstoppable Leader, you can learn many things from water. One lesson to learn from water is to be as flexible and adaptive as water.

Another lesson to learn from water is to be a powerful trailblazer and create your own leadership path and set your own course. As an Unstoppable Leader, understanding how to be flexible, adaptive, and powerful at the same time will help you persist, persevere, and overcome any life or leadership challenge or problem.

You must confront complacency, mediocrity, uncertainty, and ambiguity in your personal life before you can confront it in your professional life. You need to use the same strength and power of the unstoppable characteristics of water in order to live your core values and beliefs and blaze your own leadership path.

CHANGE

To be an Unstoppable Leader you must be a change agent. Change is a constant in life and leadership. Be proactive and begin to identify areas of opportunity in your life to change instead of waiting for them to present themselves at an inopportune time.

You must lead, manage, and deal with change daily in order to deal with it effectively. You must recognize the need for change and efficiently manage both the change and the transition.

As a change agent, you proactively cause change, transformation, growth, expansion, or improvement with an intended result in mind. It is intentional and on purpose. When you step up to be a leader, you accept the mission of being a change agent.

Flexibility and adaptability allows you to deal with the uncertainty and ambiguity of your daily leadership challenges. Learning to be flexible and adaptive allows you to become a more resilient leader. When you learn to adapt to your environment, flexing instead of breaking, you will strengthen your resiliency.

RESILIENCY

Resiliency is the ability to handle life's crises and to recover back to your normalcy. Resiliency helps you to overcome obstacles by helping you to manage stress and distress. You cannot escape difficulty, heartache, and suffering.

As a resilient person, you will experience both negative and positive emotions during challenging situations and find positive value in the challenge. However, you can become resilient in life.

Resiliency is a critical element that allows you to come back stronger than ever after crisis and chaos. An Unstoppable Leader strives to achieve results no matter the conditions. The world has changed; it is a volatile, uncertain, complex, and ambiguous environment, which means you need to prepare yourself to manage current and future challenges and opportunities.

A resilient person will find the positive aspect even in the worst of circumstances. Resiliency is the ability to persevere and rebound in the face of hardship, suffering, calamity, fears, distress, and stress.

A resilient leader takes the opportunity to leverage life's challenges and hardships as opportunities to grow, develop, and reinvent. Resiliency helps you to focus on what is important in life by clearing your heart, mind, body, and soul of junk and stress. You need to build resiliency into your life. One way to build resiliency into your life is through the Power of the Positive. Resiliency allows you to be flexible and adaptive to life's challenges and uncertain situations.

Building resiliency requires that you become proactive about your life. You need to start putting in the affects you need in your life now so you can become more resilient. Being proactive enables you to prepare for future difficulties. Being resilient will help you to be unstoppable.

Being an Unstoppable Leader requires an adaptive and resilient mindset. It is an unwavering belief in yourself, your abilities, and your capabilities. It is a belief in your unshakeable purpose and values. It is an awareness of your strengths and your challenges.

TRAIN TO WIN

When the Air Force kicked off their new physical fitness program, I went out and established a run time to see where I was in relation to the new run times. Based on my run time, waist measurement, and the sit-ups I completed, I scored an 82.

Although that score was acceptable, I was not satisfied with it. I wanted to score in the 90s and preferably 92 or higher. I needed help to achieve my goal.

I had two wingmen/mentors that helped me achieve my goals. Kevin and Brian were my two mentors who helped me train to beat the standard, not just pass it. Three times a week Kevin, Brian, and I would run 3-4 miles to develop endurance and conditioning. Besides just running, we did wind sprints and staggered the running with a jog, run, and sprint cycle.

Over a period of 18 weeks, my time went from 13:12 to 11:42. We continued to train up to the first physical assessment. On the day of the run, I finished with an 11:24 and scored a 92 on the physical assessment. We continued to run three times a week and competed in 5ks throughout the year.

The next year during my run, I finished with a 10:31. After the physical assessment, I left and went to Altus Air Force Base, Oklahoma.

Since I no longer had the benefit of my two mentors, I needed something or someone to push me to train and develop for the next year. I needed to create an effect that would help me achieve my desired outcome.

To help me continue to challenge myself and to achieve my goals, I set up the Command Chief Run for each month and gave t-shirts to anyone who could beat the Chief.

In my first six months I handed out 56 t-shirts to Airmen who beat my time. I continued this run for the two years I was assigned to Altus and my run times fell to 10:02 and finally 9:49. Mentoring and constantly challenging myself to stay in the 90s helped me to stay fit throughout my Air Force career.

Life is just like that example. It requires you to keep training, developing, and growing yourself to win. It also requires you to put a proactive effect in place to achieve your desired outcome. Here are five tips to help improve your resiliency.

- Do not become a recluse during crisis or tragedy. Being resilient is not a one-person deal. You need life-affirming relationships with close family members and friends to be resilient and healthy. When catastrophe hits you, the worst thing you can do is to seek solitude. You need people in your life to lean on during times of trouble.

- Keep the situation in perspective. Don't let the tragedy cloud your judgment or outlook on life. Seek to understand the tragedy, how it will affect your life, and do not let it control your life. Keep your eyes focused on getting through the tragedy and do not be overcome. Be an overcomer!

- Maintain your optimism. Despite the difficulty you are facing, keep a positive mindset. It will help you be resilient and help you avoid feeling negative. As you progress through the difficulty, focus on your strengths and abilities to get you through.

- Maintain a healthy lifestyle and take care of yourself. Do what you need to do to stay healthy. Get enough sleep, exercise daily, and eat healthy food. A healthy mind and body will help you be resilient and adaptive.

Being resilient, flexible, and adaptive allowed me to meet challenges and rigor during my yearlong deployment to the 386th Air Expeditionary Wing. Colonel Curlett and I had several days that exploited our flexible, adaptive, resilient, and globally aware leadership skills. Below is a snapshot of one of those days.

- 0300 Wake up, eat breakfast, head to armory for weapons

- 0500 Fly to Camp Bucca, Iraq

- 0600 Head directly to the Tactical Operations Center for mission brief

- 0700 Load up HUMVEEs, head out to start patrol

- 0800 Start dismounted IED patrol to secure convoy route

- 0930 Mounted and dismounted IED patrol complete; road and bridge secured

- 1030 Convoy passes without incident

- 1100 Start Roving Patrol

- 1300 Finish Roving Patrol and return to Base

- 1600 Fly out of Camp Bucca via Blackhawk Helicopters

- 1700 Land back at 386 AEW, return weapons to armory, shower and change clothes

- 1800 Leave base for Diwaniya to meet with government officials concerning land use issues for building dorms

- 1930 Arrive at Diwaniya, greeted by the Sheik, Government officials, Ambassador and staff, and Base General

- 1930-2130 Discussion time (chai, green tea, dates, and dinner served)

- 2300 Follow up discussion, if needed, in Shisha tent

- 0130 Depart Diwaniya

- 0300 Return to base and head to sleeping quarters

- 0700 Wake up and head to breakfast

Being an agile and adaptive leader means you must have the ability to be flexible, adaptive, and resilient during all your life and leadership challenges.

EFFECTS AND OUTCOMES

As a leader, you have a choice in how to lead and live. You can let events happen as unplanned events or by deliberate planning and preparation. Creating effects is a process of adaptive leadership. They are proactive and are not reactive. Effects are your way of achieving your desired leadership outcomes.

Using effects-based mindset thinking, you would ask yourself the following questions:

- What type of effects would be most appropriate in the given set of circumstances?

- What actions and decisions do I need to make in order to achieve team and organizational outcomes?

- What internal and external skills, abilities, talents, and resources, does my team have to help achieve the desired outcome?

- What skills, talents, abilities, and resources, do we need to learn or develop to achieve the desired outcome?

The effects mindset is a focused way to change to create the outcome or consequence that you desire. In every situation you face as a leader you can choose how to respond and what to do or not to do. Leaders who do not take the time to understand the trends and changes in our turbulent times, and fail to understand the disruptive nature of the world or marketplaces, are unprepared for the future. Change is inevitable which makes development necessary.

Adaptive leadership is a critical requirement for both military and civilian leaders in a VUCA environment. Both sets of leaders need to be concerned with national security issues of interconnected global economies and its effect on economic viability and the job market. Although this will create competition and innovation, it will also be a concern due to potential increased unemployment and persistent global market conflicts.

Additionally, with the shift in global demographics and the rise of developing countries, the dependence and competition for the world's resources will be great. The demand for energy, especially fossil and alternative fuels, will be in high demand by developed nations and emerging nations.

Finally, the speed of and pace of change, disruptive innovation, and technological advances will continue to exponentially increase each year creating uncertainty and a need for adaptive and flexible leaders who can learn quickly and act swiftly.

In an environment that is continuously in flux, a leader needs to be better educated, more adaptive, and cognitively prepared for the future challenges. A leader needs to learn adaptability in order to adjust to ever-changing leadership challenges by changing global business practices, processes, and structures.

THINKING STRATEGIES

The following thinking strategies can help you think critically under pressure and through complex and uncertain problems and challenges. The thinking strategies are time-sensitive and require an understanding of how you think and operate.

Change is a constant in a VUCA environment, and to remain successful and unstoppable you must be able to positively respond to continuous change. You must learn to have the capability to lead through continuous change and learn to be adaptive and flexible throughout problems, challenges, and situations.

IMPROVISE, ADAPT, OVERCOME

Throughout my time in the military, I have had the pleasure of working with several United States Marine Corps Senior Enlisted Leaders who taught me the value of the phrase "Improvise, Adapt, and Overcome."

The phrase emphasizes the importance of innovative and creative thinking, flexibility and adaptability, and leading in unexpected and uncertain situations. It is a vital way of thinking as a leader.

Improvise: Improvising is an essential thinking skill. In a VUCA environment, improvising is being able to create opportunities and solutions in an unexpected challenge or situation. It is a form of innovative and creative thinking that allows you to use whatever is at hand to overcome the situation.

The ability to improvise in uncertain and ambiguous situations allows you to think unconventionally and, with a degree of confidence, to meet the challenge and resolve the situation.

Adapt: The ability to adapt is another key life skill. Adaptability is the ability to be flexible and agile during changing and complex environments.

Being able to adapt to your surroundings in order to create a brighter future is a key part of adaptability. In a VUCA environment, adaptability is being flexible and adaptive to the situation and coming out stronger and more able to handle challenges.

Overcome: Overcoming is another key thinking skill which I call Victory Thinking. This is a positive mindset where you have the ability to handle and overcome any situation.

In a VUCA environment, overcoming is about creating the outcomes you want in life and positively responding to the situation. It is having the confidence to attack the situation and to be able to persevere and persist until you triumph.

REFRAME, RETHINK, REINVENT

These set of thinking skills require more time and emphasize the importance of systems, strategies, and adaptive thinking. Reframing requires you to take the time to break down the complex problem into its smallest component and relook at the problem as a system of problems to develop a solution.

Rethinking is taking the time to review and analyze what you did in the past to see if it will work again or to help develop a new solution to the problem. Finally, reinventing is a clean-sheet thinking approach to solving your problem.

Reframe: Reframing is a deliberate and reflective way of thinking to solve complex problems. It is a process of looking at a problem, not just in one way, but in several different or alternative ways.

Reframing a problem or situation allows you to think about the "What ifs" of a problem.

- What if we solve it this way versus the way we always have solved it?

- What is the outcome if we solve it this way?

Reframing takes time and requires expertise in the problem you are solving but allows you to think about creating new outcomes to known problems or situations.

In a VUCA environment, reframing a problem may help to reduce the complexity and ambiguity of the problem.

Rethink: Rethinking is a reflective way of thinking about problems and challenges. It is reviewing what you did in the past and why it worked.

Rethinking is taking the time to analyze what you did in the past and learning from the process, then using this information for future decision-making. Rethinking poses several questions in the review process.

- Why did my last approach work?

- How did it work?

- Was the outcome the one I intended?

- What steps did I use in solving the problem?

- Did I think of alternative outcomes during my thought process?

Reinvent: Reinventing is a clean-sheet approach to thinking or decision-making. The most significant outcome of clean-sheet thinking is the new perspective it brings to your decision-making. By using a clean-sheet approach, you discard your biases, predispositions, and preconceptions.

Clean-sheet thinking allows you to look at challenges and problems as if you never had seen them before. Reinventing allows you to capitalize on opportunities you may have missed during your early decision-making.

SUMMARY

Learning to be a flexible, adaptive, and resilient leader in the face of these challenges will allow you to lead successfully through adversity. You must be a flexible and adaptive leader in order to thrive.

You must recognize that change is a constant and learn to be flexible, adaptive, and responsive to change. You need to be able to lead, communicate, and operate in the extant dynamic environment. You must be flexible and adaptive to quickly respond to crisis and change.

CHARACTER CHECK

1. How adaptable are you as a leader?

2. How prepared are you to lead in a VUCA environment?

3. How resilient are you as a leader?

LOOKING INTO THE MIRROR

After reading this chapter, review and reflect on the ideas and concepts presented. Think about what opportunities, challenges, resources, or blind spots you may encounter when you begin your growth and development journey.

Use the following questions to help you grow and develop.

1. How will I incorporate this principle into my leadership development?

2. What opportunity and resources exist for me to use this principle this week, this year?

3. What blind spots may derail me from using this principle?

THE FIRST PRINCIPLES

COMMITMENT TIME

- ✓ Flexibility is the ability to adapt to new or different environments or situations

- ✓ Resiliency allows you to be flexible and adaptive to life's challenges and uncertain situations

- ✓ Learn to communicate cross-functionally and multi-culturally

- ✓ Learn to make decisions at the pace of change

- ✓ Change is inevitable which makes development necessary

- ✓ A leader needs to be able to critically analyze problems and situations and foresee second, third, and fourth order of effects of proposed policies or actions

- ✓ A leader encourages and rewards creativity, innovation, and continuous improvement

- ✓ It requires 100% of your leadership capability to lead in the world today

- ✓ Being proactive enables you to prepare for future difficulties

- ✓ Being resilient will help you to be unstoppable

THE FIRST PRINCIPLES

LEADERSHIP NOTES

CHAPTER SEVEN

THE GROWTH PRINCIPLE

DEVELOPING YOUR LEADERSHIP FOR LIFE

"One can choose to go back toward safety or forward toward growth. Growth must be chosen again and again; fear must be overcome again and again."
Abraham Maslow

In the early part of my Air Force Career, I started developing and shaping my personal leadership development program in order to prepare myself for future supervisory and leadership opportunities. Every aspect of life requires leadership and becoming a leader does not happen by accident.

I had a hunger for learning about leadership so I took every opportunity to read leadership biographies of leaders past and present, and books by Maxwell, Covey, Bennis, and Drucker, amongst others. I took every opportunity to watch how the leaders in my organization (supervisors and commanders) handled situations and challenges.

From the learning opportunities I assessed what was lacking in my development and in what areas I still needed to grow and develop. I wanted to grow, develop, and reinvent myself as a leader in order to be ready for all leadership opportunities in my career.

One of the best lessons I learned early in my career was to have a plan for lifelong learning in order to develop and grow myself. If I wanted the opportunity to be a good leader and a good supervisor, I needed to improve myself. My success is a by-product of lifelong learning.

Throughout my career, I learned about my capabilities, my values, my potential, and myself. I learned how to follow, then learned how to lead, and finally learned how to serve.

Continuous learning and continuous development creates the self-knowledge for a leader to continually reinvent their capability as a leader and a person.

REVIEW AND REFLECT

As I sat down to write this chapter, I took the time to reflect on how I grew as a leader. It truly was and is a continuous journey. As I reflected over the years of Military, Federal, and Nonprofit Leadership, a pattern of leadership growth and development emerged.

As I looked back and reflected on how I became a leader and honed my skills, I realized that it was by hard work and design. My leadership development did not just happen in a vacuum or straight-line. It occurred in phases, leaps, and stages of growth, development, and experience.

The leadership growth phases occurred through education, training, and development in the classroom, the training room, and lecture halls. The leadership leaps of growth occurred through experiences, leadership assignments, challenges, failures, and successes in leading in the work center, exercises, deployments, and the battlefield.

My leadership shaped and developed through peacetime, crisis, and conflict. This pattern of leadership growth and development is what I call the Unstoppable Leadership Growth and Development Framework.

The Unstoppable Leadership Growth and Development Framework represents what I learned over the years serving as a supervisor and frontline leader in the military and serving in leadership roles in several non-profit organizations. It represents how I developed myself and the process that molded and shaped my development as a leader.

Unstoppable Leaders understand that today's successful outcomes and results are based on yesterday's experiences and disciplined planning and preparation.

LIFELONG LEARNING

Too many times I have seen people spend more time thinking, planning, and preparing for their summer vacation than thinking, planning, and preparing for what they want to do with their life.

They meander through life and allow life's challenges and trials to shape them versus taking ownership for their life. Moreover, without a clear path to deliberately and intentionally grow and develop, they end up going through life without purpose and without direction.

A commitment to a lifelong process of learning is the key to successful leadership. In today's volatile, uncertain, complex, and ambiguous environment, learning is vital to your ability to adapt to the ever-evolving challenges and uncertainty.

Continuous learning, continuous development, and continuous growth create the self-awareness for a leader to continually reinvent their capability as a leader and a person. The process requires continuous growth, continuous development, and continuously reinventing yourself on a daily basis. This is also true in life. Leadership, learning, and life are synonymous.

Leadership requires a commitment to enduring learning. A leader knows and understands their strengths, weaknesses, capabilities, abilities, and their emotions. A leader needs self-insight into how they operate, how they make decisions, and how to treat people in order to lead people.

Today, the workplace is dependent on knowledge capital. As a leader, you need to keep that knowledge base in the organization and on your team. You can do that by building the relationship you have with your subordinates each day.

Lifelong learning is an individual and an organizational need. It is a constant reminder that learning is a lifelong process and necessary to being a better leader every day.

Continuous learning provides a leader the necessary knowledge to stay current on today's trends, but also flexible and adaptive to face tomorrow's challenges. Unstoppable Leaders continuously commit to growth, development, and reinventing themselves in order to stay at the top of their game.

REINVENTION

To achieve something that you have never achieved before, you must reinvent yourself first. You must grow and develop qualities, skills, talents, and characteristics that you do not have today. You must learn to be flexible and adaptive to become that new person.

To become truly successful in reinventing yourself, you need to clarify where you want to go, establish a plan, and write it down. Learn about your skills and capabilities and take control of your life and leadership. This is the key to becoming a better leader.

A leader must know and understand their strengths, weaknesses, capabilities, abilities, and their emotions. Knowledge-enabled leaders in an organization provide the necessary competitive edge needed to strive in the global marketplace.

You must continue to develop this area of expertise as you grow your professional expertise. You must continue to grow your team and organizational leadership skills, attitude, aptitude, and leadership experiences. You live in a complex world and you are bombarded 24 hours a day with continuous data and information. This constant and continuous flow of data creates opportunities for gaining knowledge.

Leadership success comes to the leader who is best prepared to gather the data and information and then transfers the knowledge into useable and actionable wisdom. If you want to grow, develop, and reinvent as a leader, it is critical to be a lifelong learner. Leadership is the difference between success and just surviving.

To succeed in our volatile, complex, ambiguous world, you have no choice but to master your ability to adapt and learn. To be an Unstoppable Leader you need to grow, develop, and change yourself every year through the eight disciplines of personal development.

UNSTOPPABLE LEADERSHIP GROWTH AND DEVELOPMENT FRAMEWORK

The Unstoppable Leadership Growth and Development Framework represents what I learned serving as a supervisor and frontline leader in the military and serving in leadership roles in several non-profit organizations. It represents how I developed myself and the process that molded and shaped my development as a leader.

Each phase, leap, and stage allowed me to become the leader I needed to be for each new assignment and each new challenge. Through the use of a common leadership framework, all aspects of my leadership development and individual progress was measured.

LAYING THE FOUNDATION

The growth phases of my leadership laid the foundation for developing my leadership and provided a solid foundation of understanding of leadership and being a leader. It provided me the knowledge and awareness of characteristics, competencies, and expectations of a leader.

This growth phase was and is the underlying foundation of my leadership. It can also be defined as lifelong learning provided by continuous learning, education, and training.

The Air Force provided advanced education and targeted training for strategic senior enlisted leaders. This targeted education and training developed enterprise structure and perspective, building and sustaining relationships, government organization and processes, strategic communication, managing organizations and resources, change management, continuous improvement, strategic thinking, vision, and decision-making.

The advanced educational courses as described are:

- The Center for Creative Leadership Development Program enhances senior enlisted leaders' leadership capabilities through extensive assessment, group discussions, self-reflection, small group activities, and personal coaching

- The Gettysburg Leadership Experience course expands on participants' improved knowledge about themselves and their leadership ability; it brings into sharper focus the dual role of the leader and the follower

- The Air Force Enterprise Management Seminar provides a collaborative and powerfully engaging opportunity for senior enlisted leaders to increase their effectiveness

- The Air Force Smart Operations for the 21st Century Executive Leadership Course augments senior leaders' existing leadership skills with an understanding of how to manage performance and strategically align continuous process improvement

The Air Force designed courses increased my leadership effectiveness and technical competence each step of my career path. When it came time for me to choose my bachelor's degree and my master's degree, I focused on those degrees that increased my leadership effectiveness and technical competence. I aligned my personal growth and development goals with my chosen profession.

LEADERSHIP INSIGHT

In order to get ahead in your work, in your life, or as a leader, you need to commit to deliberate and continuous learning. This is an indispensable element of leadership.

- What do you need to learn to grow to the next level?

- What leadership skills or management techniques will help you be more effective?

- What leadership courses will help you be a more effective leader?

- What skills and abilities will increase your technical competence?

This alignment allowed me to increase my value to the organization and increased my potential for promotion. It also ensured that I had the right skills, capabilities, and abilities for the increased responsibility required for the next leadership and next technical level. I prepared myself by growing myself toward the next opportunity instead of waiting for the next opportunity to show up.

THE FIRST PRINCIPLES

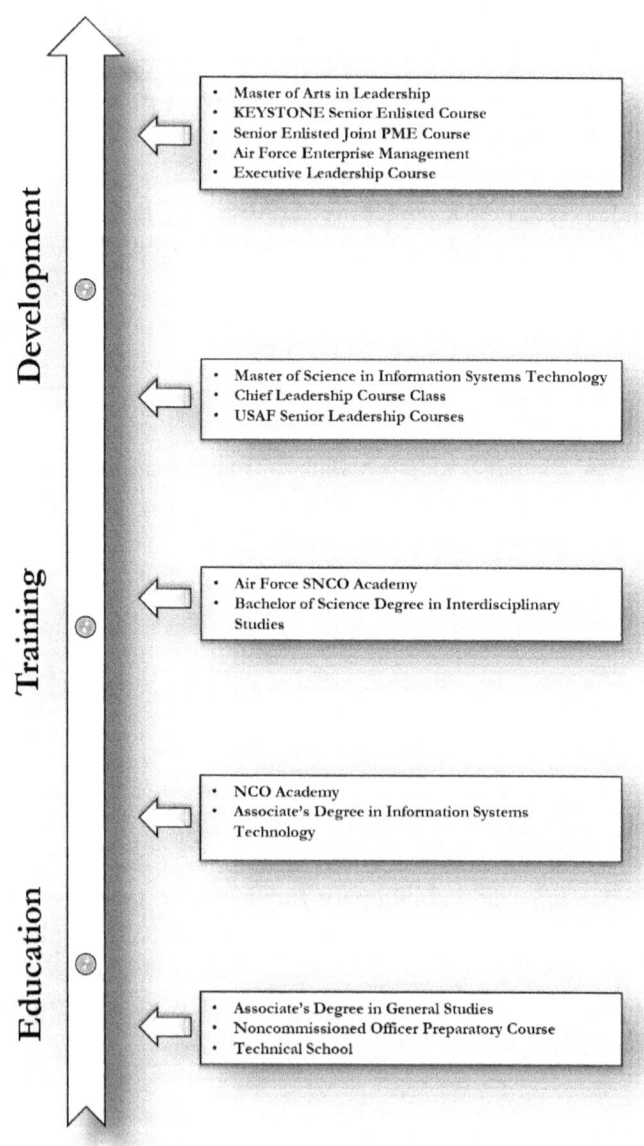

LEAPS OF GROWTH

The growth stages of my leadership occurred through developmental assignments, leadership opportunities, and gained experiences.

These three areas provided leaps of leadership growth by challenging me to apply, adapt, and refine my leadership knowledge and understanding into a working philosophy.

They allowed me the time to test, experiment, and practice the art of leadership in order to master my leadership role.

Assignments, challenges, and gained experiences forced me out of my comfort zones and forced me to rethink and reframe my approach to leadership.

Unstoppable Leaders continuously reinvent themselves through a process of continuous development and continuous growth.

Assignments: Early in my career, my responsibility was to become the technical expert and learn everything I could about my specific job--Computer Operations. As I advanced in rank I took on the responsibility of shift supervisor and directing operations on the Computer Room floor.

Becoming a supervisor taught me the responsibility of leading other Airmen. It grew my leadership skills of empathy, goal setting, and discipline. As I continued to advance in rank and changed bases of assignments, I assumed more responsibilities, took care of more Airmen, and gained more experiences.

- Computer Operator, 2166th Communications Squadron, 10th Tactical Reconnaissance Wing, Royal Air Force Alconbury, United Kingdom **(Entry-level position/Tactical Leadership)**

- Non-Commissioned Officer in Charge, Computer Operations and Training, 6th Missile Warning Squadron, Cape Cod Air Force Station **(Journeyman position/Tactical Leadership)**

- Chief, Communications, Computers, Command and Control Systems Security, Air Force Flight Test Center **(Journeyman position/Operational Leadership)**

- Chief, Information Assurance, 612th Air Communications Squadron, Davis-Monthan Air Force Base **(Operational Leadership)**

- Deployed to Taif, Saudi Arabia, in support of Operation Southern Watch, Superintendent, Information Assurance **(Operational Leadership)**

- Superintendent, Information Systems Flight, 52nd Communications Squadron, Spangdahlem Air Base, Germany **(Operational/Strategic Leadership)**

- Deployed to Italy in support of Determined Force and Sky Anvil, Superintendent, Wing Initial Communications Package **(Operational Leadership)**

- Superintendent, United States Air Forces In Europe Information Assurance, United States Air Forces in Europe Computer Support Squadron, Ramstein Air Base, Germany **(Strategic Leadership)**

- Superintendent, Wing Information Assurance, Superintendent, Network Control Center, Superintendent, Information Systems Flight, 786th Communications Squadron, Ramstein Air Base, Germany **(Operational/Strategic Leadership)**

- Deployed to Kuwait in support of Operation Southern Watch, Superintendent, Information Assurance **(Operational Leadership)**

- Command Computer and Communications Functional Manager, Communications and Information Directorate, Headquarters United States Air Forces in Europe, Ramstein Air Base, Germany **(Strategic Leadership)**

- Command Chief Master Sergeant, 97th Air Mobility Wing, Altus Air Force Base **(Strategic Leadership)**

- Command Chief Master Sergeant, 386th Air Expeditionary Wing, Ali Al Salem Air Base **(Strategic Leadership)**

- Command Chief Master Sergeant, 14th Air Force/Air Forces Strategic and Joint Functional Component Command for Space, Vandenberg Air Force Base **(Strategic Leadership)**

- Command Senior Enlisted Leader, United States Strategic Command, Offutt Air Force Base **(Strategic Leadership)**

Assignments gave me the opportunity to practice the knowledge and education I learned and to put it into action.

The learning I received through the actual application of leadership exponentially grew my capabilities and decision-making and helped me move to the next stage in my leadership.

Each of these leaps of growth launched me to the next leadership stage and provided me the knowledge to handle each challenge.

Challenges: A leadership challenge is just an opportunity for a leader to excel at their craft. Each assignment provided new challenges and new opportunities to grow and refine my leadership from tactical to operational to strategic leadership levels.

- Responsible for the direction, professional development, and morale of 215 personnel. Advised and assisted the Commander in providing program management, logistics support, and implementation of military plans.

- Directly oversaw the enlisted professional development programs, military readiness, and mission effectiveness of 1,500 enlisted personnel.

- Provided direction and oversight to 192 senior enlisted personnel concerning long-range plans and concepts, and budget recommendation for the development of the enlisted force.

- Oversaw the health, morale, welfare, training, fitness, operations tempo, and utilization of 13,500 forces to include Navy, Japanese, Korean, and Australian coalition partners.

- Oversaw the utilization, professional development, military readiness, and mission effectiveness of 12,000 personnel assigned to 155 units at 44 worldwide locations.

- Directly oversaw the enlisted professional development programs, military readiness, and mission effectiveness of 18,560 Marine, Army, Navy, and Air Force enlisted personnel in 128 worldwide locations.

Experiences: The key to my growth and development was the ability, willingness, and hunger to be the best. Experiences grow you as a leader exponentially and dramatically. Your experiences are the result of your leadership words and behaviors in action.

- Conducted Senior Leader Engagements with visiting Congressional Delegations, Joint Senior Leaders, State Governors, Foreign Dignitaries, and local government officials.

- Coordinated and worked strategic alliances and partnerships with Air Force, Army, Navy, and Joint Functional Component Command and International Senior Enlisted Leaders.

- Conducted Mil-to-Mil Engagements for the Partnership for Peace initiative.

- Senior Mentor for the National Defense University KEYSTONE program Senior Enlisted leader professional and leadership development program. Department of Defense Senior Enlisted Leader Council member.

- Air Force Enlisted Board of Directors member and Force Development Council member.

THE FIRST PRINCIPLES

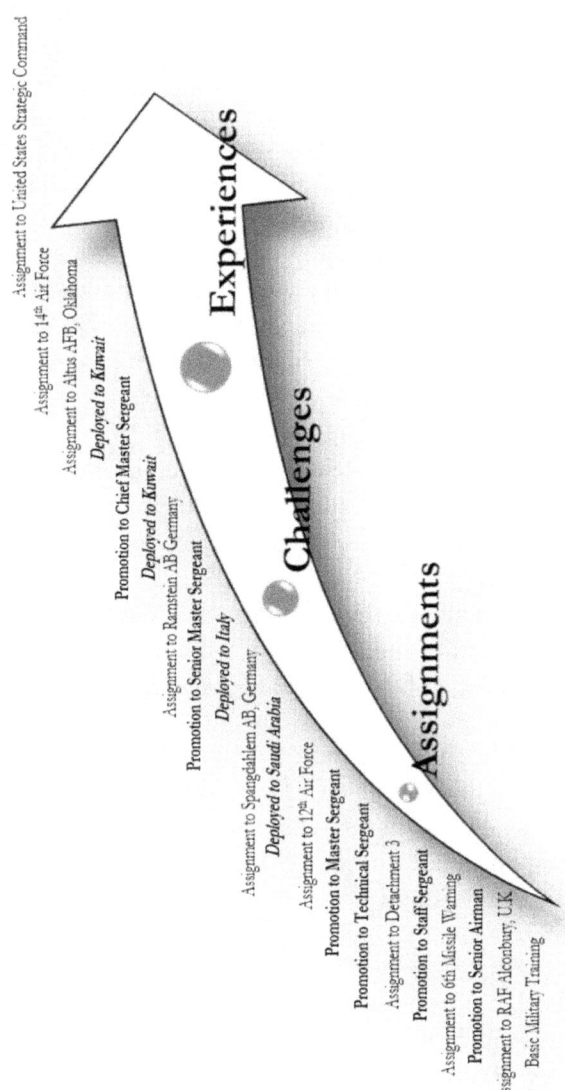

LEADERSHIP STAGES AND LEVELS

The Leadership Stages and Levels indicate each stage of growth and development you go through as you become a better and more effective leader.

Each level of leadership--tactical, operational, and strategic--indicates the level of leader you need to grow to.

I transitioned through each stage as my leadership knowledge, awareness, and insight increased. Each of the phases and the leaps of growth provided me the ability to grow, stretch, and develop.

- Each progressive stage provided more experience in leading myself, teams, and organizations

- Each stage provided a better understanding of human capital strategies, team development, and organizational change management

Self-Leadership: Before you can lead others, you need to learn to lead yourself. This begins with the self-awareness of your strengths, weaknesses, capabilities, abilities, and your emotions. You must know yourself first and understand how you operate before you can lead effectively.

To be a great leader you need to understand who you are and how you operate as a human being first before you can lead others.

Inexperienced Leader: This is your first venture into the leadership realm after you learn to lead yourself. You may have a knowledge base of leadership to develop and apply your own leadership style, but you lack the experience to appreciate the dynamics of leadership. You seek out opportunities for more experiences to harden your core skills.

Emerging Leader: The seed of leadership begins to grow and the foundation of your leadership begins to take root in your life. As an emerging leader, you need time to build your personal, professional, and leadership core competencies to establish rings of growth and development.

You are establishing well-developed interpersonal skills with proven ability to lead, motivate, and inspire cross-functional teams to meet and surpass objectives.

Experienced Leader: You start to grow and expand the boundaries of your leadership. As an experienced leader, you continue to build a solid foundation in your leadership core competencies to ensure you are well rooted in your skills.

You experience successes and failures as a leader and have learned valuable lessons that you can use as a leader. As an experienced leader, you continue to seek out opportunities for your growth and development and for opportunities to use your skills to sharpen your capability.

Unstoppable Leader: The signs of growth and development are present, and maturity of your leadership is evident. You have years of growth, development, experience, and life lessons that have honed your Unstoppable Leadership skills, talents, and abilities.

THREE LEVELS OF LEADERSHIP

Tactical: The tactical level is the first form of leadership. It is learning to lead you first. Learning to lead and manage your life is the critical first step in leadership. You must be able to control and regulate yourself in order to lead others.

Operational: The operational level is leading teams or leading others. It is the next level of leadership and is necessary in order to accomplish the organizational mission.

With operational leadership, you have the ability to influence the growth and development of two or more people which is a critical leadership role in any organization.

Strategic: The strategic level is leading in an organization or leading the organization.

Strategic leadership spans across many teams, divisions, or directorates, and here you have the ability to influence a multitude of people.

Through a disciplined approach, you accept responsibility and accountability for your decisions and actions, which allow you the freedom to accept your failures and successes equally.

THE FIRST PRINCIPLES

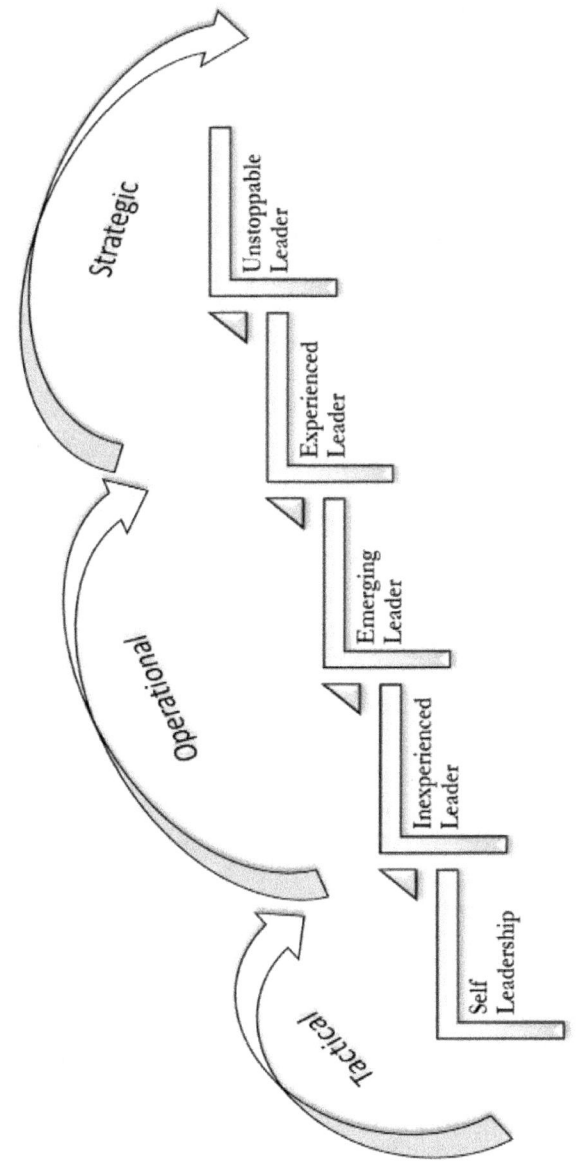

THE COMPLETE MODEL

The one thing you will notice very quickly from the complete framework model is that this does not just happen overnight and it takes hard work and discipline to grow and develop as a leader. The Unstoppable Leadership Growth and Development Framework is a disciplined and thoughtful approach to growing and developing yourself as a leader and provides you a solid leadership foundation to be a valuable leader in any organization.

Who you are as a leader is more important than how you lead. So, as you grow, develop, and reinvent yourself as a leader, you need to be disciplined and thoughtful in your approach to developing your inner core and your authentic character.

The other thing you will notice is that as you move up in the organization you will need more training, development, and experience to be a flexible and adaptive leader. The higher you go up in an organization, the more strategic your view is and your enterprise understanding must be.

As you begin to attain more operational and strategic experience in developing vision, strategy, policy development, conflict resolution, budget cost controls, performance recognition programs, and performance plans for your team, the greater asset you are for your organization. Through a disciplined approach you prepare yourself for opportunities that you would not have if you lived life in a laissez faire manner.

THE FIRST PRINCIPLES

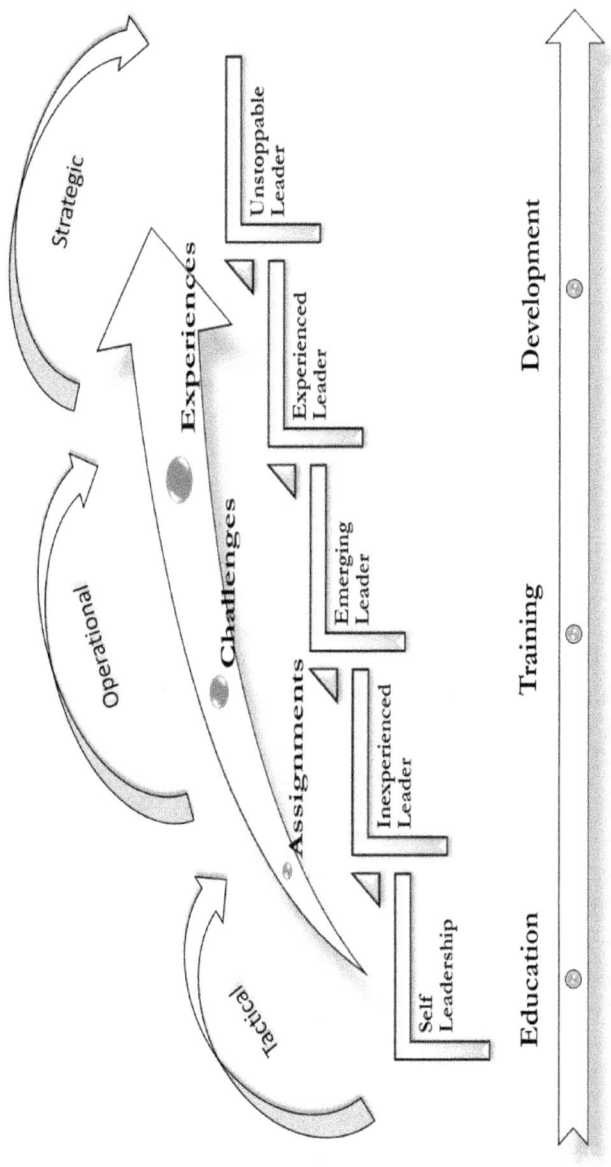

THE UNSTOPPABLE TORTOISE

Aesop's tale, The Tortoise and the Hare, is a great analogy of an unstoppable approach to the journey of life and leadership and is a good illustration of the complete Unstoppable Leadership Growth and Development Roadmap.

The two main characters of the story are the tortoise and the hare. The hare is an overconfident and arrogant braggart, while the tortoise is disciplined and unassuming.

The hare incessantly crows about his natural abilities, talents, and skills to anyone who will listen. The hare teases and taunts the tortoise because he is slow, methodical, and not prone to whimsy.

The tortoise is an easy target for the hare. Unlike the hare, the tortoise is self-confident and self-assured in his ability, but does not brag on his abilities, talents, and skills.

When the race starts, the hare is off quickly and is far ahead of the plodding tortoise. With an overwhelming lead, the hare makes hasty and unwise decisions to nap and eat instead of winning the race. The tortoise continues with his personal goal to win the race and is not distracted or deterred. In the end, the hare's decisions cost him the race and his pride.

To me, the hare represents a person with natural gifts and talents who uses them in an undisciplined and frivolous manner. The hare takes for granted his endowed talents, abilities, and skills and does not use a disciplined approach to hone them for future use.

The hare also makes a critical mistake at the start of the race. He sees the race as a sprint to the finish instead of a journey. The hare, who has goaded the tortoise into the race and bragged to all the animals that he can beat the tortoise, fails to set a goal to win the race and instead assumes he will win.

Repeatedly in the story, the hare makes life choices without a full understanding of the second, third, and fourth order of effects of those decisions. His failure to understand the effects and outcomes of his decisions is why he fails to win the race.

The tortoise, on the other hand, realizes that he must build upon what he is gifted with and grow, develop, and reinvent himself to be unstoppable. He realizes that this race is a life journey and not a sprint and in order to win he cannot rely just on talent.

The tortoise does not possess the talents and capabilities of the hare, but during his journey, he hones and forges the talents and skills he needs to win. At the beginning of the race he systematically and logically sets a long-term goal to win the race despite the capabilities of the hare.

All of his decisions and actions point to one goal-- win the race of life. The tortoise's 8P Focus gives him an unstoppable purpose and a single-mindedness of action.

He establishes actionable goals, makes well thought out decisions, and takes deliberate actions to achieve his victory. Through his persistence, perseverance, and performance he overcomes the odds and wins the race.

UNSTOPPABLE LEADERSHIP STRATEGIC FUNDAMENTALS MAP

The Unstoppable Leadership Strategic Fundamentals Map is a visual display of those key and essential leadership foundations that I feel a leader needs to lead effectively. The fundamentals are derived from my own reflection and review of past leadership experiences and practices.

Over time, each of these fundamentals were ingrained into how I operated as a leader of myself, of other people, and in my organizations. The Strategic Fundamentals Map correlates to the Unstoppable Model and focuses on the characteristics of who a leader is in their inner core and focuses on the attributes leaders need to lead.

Each fundamental describes a part or component of the leadership experience. Leadership fundamentals influence how you perform as a leader, how you interact with people, and how welll you lead in an organization.

The Unstoppable Leadership Strategic Fundamentals Map is a leadership guide for you to review and reflect on throughout your leadership experience.

THE FIRST PRINCIPLES

Unstoppable Leadership Fundamentals

Performance Analysis	Leadership Performance	Leadership Focus	Leadership Strategy	Leadership Thinking	Leadership Attitude	Leadership Character	Leadership Drivers
Reflect	Decisions	Planning	Vision	Strategic	Positive	Authentic	Purpose
Review	Actions	Preparation	Mission	Collaborative	Optimistic	Credible	Values
Rework	Effects	Insight	Goals	Divergent	Resilient	Responsible	Beliefs
Reject	Impact	Foresight	Objectives	Convergent	Passionate	Accountable	Worldview
Receive	Outcomes	Perspective	Tactics	Creative	Disciplined	Trustworthy	Experiences

The use of the fundamentals map provides a common leadership catalog and promotes a common understanding of the key foundational elements of a leader. These fundamentals represent the leadership characteristics that a leader must practice to be Unstoppable.

Each foundation is comprised of singular elements that reinforce the overall leadership fundamentals. Each foundation can be broken down into primary elements.

For example, the key primary elements of Fundamental Leadership Drivers are:

- Purpose – What drives you each day? The "Why" of your life and leadership.

- Values – What core values do you hold dear?

- Beliefs – What are your beliefs? Do they limit you are expand you?

- Worldview – What lenses do you see the world through?

- Experiences – How has your leaf and leadership experiences molded and shaped you?

The fundamentals map provides you a holistic way to breakdown key elements of leadership to see how they fit together to shape your leadership. It also provides you a way to think about how well you are leading and what elements of leadership require further growth and development.

UNSTOPPABLE LEADERSHIP STRATEGIC ACTION STRUCTURE

In my book *You are Unstoppable,* I discuss that you are the key to your destiny and that in order to succeed in life you need to lead yourself first and then you need to take action.

You have to lead yourself purposefully and intentionally. You have to lead yourself out of your comfort zones to experience real growth and development.

You are the chief driver and architect of your leadership. As the chief driver and architect you have the ability and capability to create the outcomes in your life and your leadership and have the impact you want. You can become an Unstoppable Leader only through the desire and passion from within yourself.

An example of how the components fit together can be seen in the Unstoppable Leadership Strategic Action Structure. This structure is made up of those parts of the Leadership Fundamentals that drive and shape your decisions, outcomes, and consequences. Each component describes a part of the leadership experience.

THE FIRST PRINCIPLES

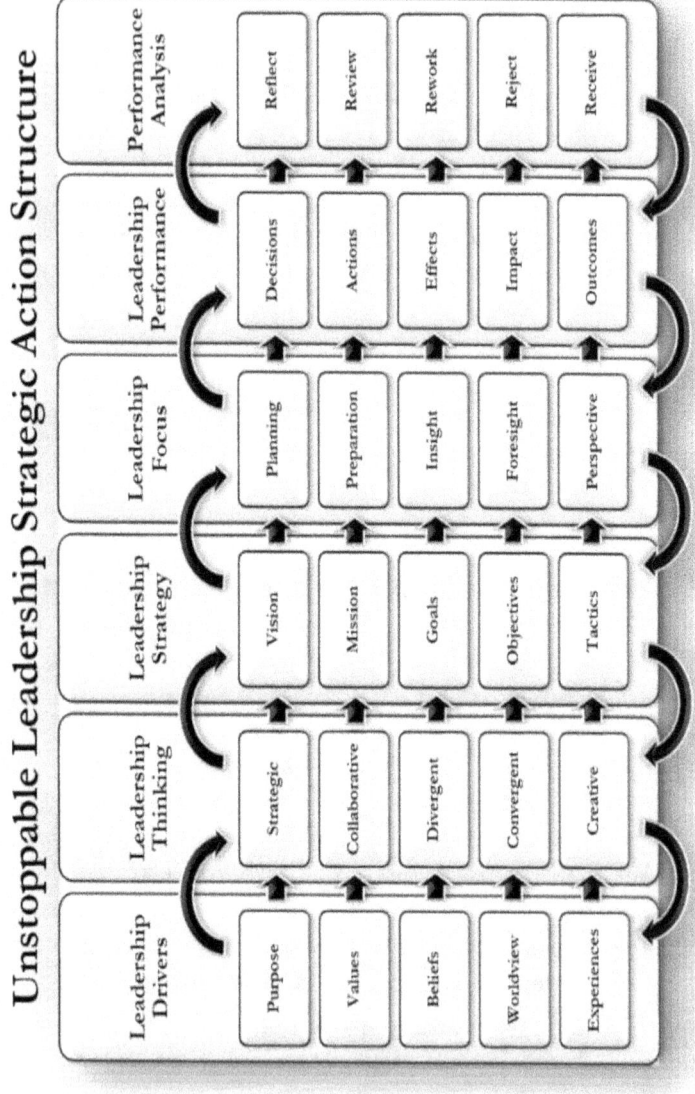

GROWING INTO YOUR LEADERSHIP

At the beginning of each New Year, take the opportunity to establish new leadership goals and create new opportunities. In order to get ahead in your work, in your life, or as a leader, you need to commit to deliberate and continuous learning. As a leader, you need to ask yourself:

- What do I need to learn today to be a better leader?

- What leadership skills or management techniques will help me be more effective?

- What are my blind spots that I need to fix?

Significant opportunities of personal growth and success will arise throughout your lifetime. If you are ready to make positive changes and new breakthroughs in your life, you will need to embrace these opportunities and grow as a leader.

Successful leaders are committed to lifelong learning; they are continuously developing, growing, and reinventing themselves. They are continually preparing for even greater opportunities in life and leadership. They never stop preparing for the day when their leadership opportunities arrive. A plan and strategy begins first with an understanding of who you are. What skills, talents, experiences, and attitude for learning do you possess, and can you use them to build yourself up as a leader?

Purposeful development and self-assessment are keys to continual growth as a leader. Although this list of questions is not all conclusive, they can help you to determine what your leadership needs are.

Furthermore, as you read the questions, other questions may come to mind that may help your leadership needs assessment to be completed. Write them down and answer them too.

- Do I have a leadership development plan?

- Do I have the ability to organize ideas, resources, and time effectively?

- Do I have the ability to make critical decisions?

- Do I have the ability to trust others and delegate work effectively?

- Do I have the desire to mentor, coach, and teach my people?

- Do I have a strong desire to make an impact within my organization?

- Am I successful at building a team and developing their skills?

- Do I have the ability to develop leadership growth plans for my people?

- Can I give clear guidance to achieve goals?

- Can I influence others to achieve the organization's mission?

- Do I seek out opportunities to grow and develop my leadership skills?

After you determine your leadership needs, you need to align them with the Eight Disciplines of Personal Development and design your plan against them and create your leadership growth and development plan. To be an Unstoppable Leader you need to grow, develop, and change yourself every year through the eight disciplines of personal development.

EIGHT DISCIPLINES OF PERSONAL DEVELOPMENT

You must develop and grow yourself as a leader in the Eight Disciplines of Personal Development of the Unstoppable Model. These areas of development help you grow and develop holistically and congruently. The eight areas are developed and grown through personal insight and personal mastery.

Personal: This discipline is You the Person. This discipline focuses on who you are--your purpose, values, character, and worldview. This discipline is also focused on how you communicate, show respect and extend dignity to others, build relationships, live with integrity and trust, and how resilient you are in your life.

Questions for Growth--What do you want to do to learn to express yourself authentically? What do you need to do to pursue new friends and encounter new people? What do you want to do to enjoy your family relationships more?

Professional: This discipline is concerned with you, your career, and the skills needed to succeed. This discipline focuses on your experience, technical skills, management skills, talents, and aptitudes. This discipline also focuses on the necessary education, training, and development you need to remain competent in your expertise.

Questions for Growth--What do you want to achieve in your career, or what do you want to achieve in your profession? What development and growth skills do you want to gain?

Leadership: This discipline focuses on your leadership skills, attitude, aptitude, leadership experience, and overall development. This discipline also focuses on your leadership opportunities, building alliances and partnerships, leadership authenticity, selfless service attitude, talent development, and culture creation.

Questions for Growth--What leadership skills do you need to develop? What teambuilding skills do you need to develop? What inventories or assessments do you need to take to discover your leadership development needs?

Spiritual: This discipline focuses on you seeking and finding personal meaning and purpose for your life through soul-searching, prayer, and meditation. This discipline also focuses on strengthening your beliefs, principles, and values to sustain you as a person through self-awareness and self-discovery.

Questions for Growth--What do you want to study, explore, or practice about spiritualism, your faith, or another religion? How will this help you to build resiliency into your life?

Emotional: This discipline focuses on you managing your life's challenges in a positive, optimistic way by demonstrating self-control, personal fortitude, and moral character. It is about harnessing the power of managing emotions.

Questions for Growth--What fears do you want to overcome? What do you want to learn in order to control or manage your emotions?

Physical: This discipline focuses on your understanding of how your personal wellness and wellbeing effects your personal growth, development, and ability to function daily.

Questions for Growth--What are the health/physical goals you want to achieve? What healthy habits do you need to incorporate into your life?

Mental: This discipline is about your intellectual and mental health capacity. This discipline focuses on your intellectual growth, mental activities, and your creative and critical thinking.

Questions for Growth--Is there any specific information or knowledge you want to gain? What new mindsets do you want to develop that will help you in your life?

Social: This discipline focuses on developing and sustaining trustworthy, valued relationships and friendships. To get a comprehensive, balanced study of all-important areas in your life, you need to ask yourself where you need to improve each of the eight disciplines of personal growth.

Questions for Growth--What do you currently do for your community? Are you part of a volunteer organization or do you volunteer your time to help others? How many hours per week do you volunteer?

The beginning of your Unstoppable Leadership starts with the knowledge that you are the owner of your success, destiny, and leadership legacy. That knowledge begins when you methodically and purposefully grow and develop your life and leadership each year with a 12-month Life and Leadership plan.

SAMPLE 12-MONTH LIFE AND LEADERSHIP PLAN

A leadership growth and development plan is a roadmap of where you are as a leader and where you want to go in your career and in life. It is a disciplined and focused method to chart, plan, prepare, and execute your life and leadership development. Below is an example of a developmental plan.

- Personal – Inspiring My Self
- Professional – Creating Capacity in My Life
- Leadership – Building and Discovering Self
- Spiritual – Discovering God
- Emotional – Overcoming Fear and Controlling My Emotions
- Physical – Building My Physical Self
- Mental – Building Resiliency
- Social – Sharing My Life

SUMMARY

You should think about how to be a lasting leader and not a temporary success. You want to grow, develop, and reinvent yourself so you are built to stand the trials and challenges of leadership and not wither under the stresses and strains.

You need to develop and grow yourself daily. The Unstoppable Leadership Fundamentals are those key and essential leadership elements that drive and shape your leadership.

CHARACTER CHECK

1. What are you doing to grow, develop, and reinvent yourself?

2. How seriously do you view lifelong learning and development?

3. How well do you lead in the tactical, operational, and strategic realms of leadership?

LOOKING INTO THE MIRROR

After reading this chapter, review and reflect on the ideas and concepts presented. Think about what opportunities, challenges, resources, or blind spots you may encounter when you begin your growth and development journey.

Use the following questions to help you grow and develop.

1. How will I incorporate this principle into my leadership development?

2. What opportunity and resources exist for me to use this principle this week, this year?

3. What blind spots may derail me from using this principle?

COMMITMENT TIME

- ✓ You are responsible for your growth and development

- ✓ Growth and development are not a one-time event, they are continuous and deliberate

- ✓ Seek to achieve mastery of your life and leadership to lead and dare greatly

- ✓ Leadership is a performance art, so create a masterpiece out of your life

- ✓ Perseverance, planning, preparation, persistence, and resilience are keys to your growth and development

- ✓ Give yourself the time to discover your life's passion

- ✓ Growing and developing yourself begins from an inward desire to change; you must be your own change agent

- ✓ Clarify your leadership strategy and life vision

- ✓ Seek to continuously reinvent yourself

- ✓ Seek to continuously grow yourself

- ✓ Seek to continuously develop yourself

THE FIRST PRINCIPLES

LEADERSHIP NOTES

CHAPTER EIGHT

THE ALIGNMENT PRINCIPLE

THE CRITICAL FUSION OF YOUR PERSONAL AND PROFESSIONAL LIFE

(CV x OV)
A fusion of your core values and the values of the organization
Inspire or Retire Theorem
Thomas Narofsky
F(X) Leadership Unleashed

One of the first pieces of advice I received from my fellow Chief Master Sergeants after I was selected for promotion to Chief Master Sergeant was:

> Remember, as Chief Master Sergeant and an Air Force Senior Enlisted Leader you have a target on your back. You must never ever forget that you are always on stage, and how you live your life and

how you lead will be under the critical eye of your people. Leadership is a choice, so each day you will need to decide what kind of leader you will be. Always, always, always choose to be a leader of integrity. Integrity means living by your word, keeping your promises, and over-delivering in everything you do.

You must lead by example and set the standard for others to follow each day. Your core values need to constantly mirror the Air Force Core Values. Never forget that leadership is all about people and the mission. If you lead your people and treat them as valuable members of your team, they will accomplish the mission.

This was great advice and a good reminder to never forget that I was always on stage as a leader and my team and organization was looking at me to set the example as a senior enlisted leader.

In Air Force Instruction 36-2618, *The Enlisted Force Structure*, the Air Force establishes high standards and expectations for all leaders. Below are key leader and leadership expectations:

- Clearly meet, and strive to exceed, the standards and expectations levied upon all junior enlisted Airmen and Non-Commissioned Officers.

- Epitomize excellence, professionalism, pride, and competence, serving as a role model for all Airmen to emulate.

- Demonstrate, inspire, and develop in others an internalized understanding of Air Force Core Values and The Airman's Creed.

- Epitomize the finest qualities of a military leader. Provide highly effective leadership. A Senior Non-Commissioned Officer's primary purpose is mission accomplishment.

- Lead and manage teams while maintaining the highest level of readiness to ensure mission success.

- As a key mentor, you must deliberately develop subordinates into enlisted leaders of the future.

As a senior leader, I was accountable and was expected to lead by example, set the standard, and then live it daily. This was a 24 hour, 7 days a week, and 365 days a year leadership responsibility. It required 100% of my effort; nothing less would do.

As a way to mitigate the risk of not living up to the Air Force Standard and setting the wrong example for my team and organization, I aligned my core values with the Air Force Core values and high leadership standards for myself and my teams.

By demanding excellence in my life and leadership, I was always striving to be better than the standard. This is critical for you to understand as a leader--your leadership is always under scrutiny by your people.

People are looking to see if your words and actions are congruent. They look to see how you show up to work each day. They look to see how you live your life away from work. They are looking to see if you are authentic and aligned with the organization. They look to see if your life and leadership are authentic.

How you lead each day is a choice, so ask yourself these questions at the beginning of each day:

- How will I be perceived when I walk through the office door? (Perceptions are reality in the eye of the beholder.)

- Am I the same person at work and at home or am I living two different lives? (Authentic Leader)

ALIGNMENT

Alignment is the fusion or synchronization of the combined values, beliefs, and tenets of you and the organization. Each of us spends a good portion of our lives at work and based on the Bureau of Labor, we spend 8.7 hours a day at work, this equates to over 100,000 hours after 50 years.

Core values are an important part of organizational culture. An organizational leader must lead by example and reinforce the organizational core values. With that in mind, would it not make sense to work for a company or an organization that aligns with your personal core values, beliefs, and worldview?

Life is too short to live without passion and to lead unaligned. You need to work for an organization that you can be passionate about going to work to each day and making an impact!

DO THE GROUND WORK FIRST

I have attended numerous Air Shows and have marveled at the teamwork and precision of the Air Force Thunderbirds, the Navy Blue Angels, and the Royal Air Force Red Arrows. This teamwork and precision is displayed in the air through their aerial acrobatics, but the real teamwork and precision begins on the ground.

The team members trust and rely on each other to perform close maneuvers and to perform death defying stunts. To perform these death defying stunts requires an enormous amount of trust between each team member.

This trust is built upon an alignment of their Service core values and the 7Cs of each member. The trust relationship is built upon each person trusting in the character, competence, courage, commitment and choices of each pilot flying the jet next to them.

They trust and rely on each other for honesty and integrity (Character), they have the skills and talents to fly and maneuver (Competence), they have the nerve and daring to fly dangerously close (Courage), they are steadfast to performing together (Commitment), and they have a keen ability to make quick and precise decisions during each maneuver (Choices).

Without the groundwork to build the trust relationship, the team could not perform and soar in the clouds. When your core values, the team's core values, and the organization's core values are aligned, it gives you the ability to perform and reach new heights of achievement.

ALIGNED VALUES

The best way for you to lead is from a position of leadership strength--your values. The surest way for you to lead from a position of strength is to ensure your values and the organization's values are aligned. It is a melding of your leadership and the leadership expectations of the organization.

Because your values play a critical part in your life, you need to work for an organization that you feel complements your values. Being able to work for an organization that aligns with your values will help to increase your loyalty and respect for the organization.

When your values are aligned, you feel inspired and motivated to give your full potential to the organization. When your values are aligned, you feel energized, enthusiastic, empowered, and eager to make an impact in your organization. An organizational leader must lead by example and reinforce the organizational core values.

Why are aligned values important?

- Values drive leadership decisions
- Values drive a leader's behavior

- Values drive employee decisions

- Values drive employee behaviors

- Values drive organizational culture

The culture of an organization is an expression of aligned values. When the organizational and personal values are aligned, the organization and its people thrive. Long-term success for an organization is built upon the alignment between personal and organizational values.

The Air Force's core values are Integrity First, Service Before Self, and Excellence in All We Do. These core values are the solid foundation upon which Air Force Leadership stands on.

My #1 core value is Integrity. As an Air Force Senior Enlisted leader I needed to model and maintain the values of the organization and act in a way that indicated that my leadership was congruent and aligned to the Air Force Core Values. I needed to walk the walk and be authentic.

When personal and organizational core values are aligned, then they are driving in the same direction and you can unleash the full potential of your leadership and your organization.

Organizational leaders are the primary source in an organization that determines the values and culture of the organization.

THE FIRST PRINCIPLES

The leader sets the tone and mood of an organization's culture and work environment. Through the leader's words and actions, he lives out the culture he wants the organization to follow. Leading with your purpose and your core values ensures your life and leadership are congruent.

Individual values that are congruent with an organization's values may help to strengthen organizational identification and a sense of organizational pride.

Team members may have values that are in conflict with organizational values which then creates conflict. A lack of values alignment or congruence can cause stress, tension, or conflict in your life until you realign yourself to your purpose, values, and beliefs.

When personal and organizational values are divergent or misaligned, you and the organization are pulling in the wrong direction and productivity decreases. Unstoppable Leaders model and maintain their values and act in a way that is both honest and congruent with their values and their organization's values.

My first real taste of misaligned leadership values was in 2004 when I arrived at Altus Air Force Base as the new Wing Command Chief.

It was during my onboarding phase that I encountered several leaders that were concerned more about themselves versus taking care of their people. After sitting down with them and listening to their complaints, it became very evident that their values were misaligned with the needs of the Air Force.

I could tell immediately they were concerned more about ME (self-centeredness) than their team or the organization and they were focused only on their problems and not on making an impact. A leader who is concerned more about ME is a cancer in an organization.

They also blamed others for their lack of promotion versus accepting responsibility for their personal and professional decisions and choices. There were two things I did after these counseling sessions to reinforce the standards, roles, and responsibilities that leaders in the organization must live up to and emulate.

First, through one-on-one counseling sessions and frequent organizational meetings, we discussed the importance of leadership and the role of leadership. The second thing I did was to create two visual reminders of these responsibilities: the S.T.RI.P.E.S. poster and the Inspire or Retire Theorem.

S.T.R.I.P.E.S.

The S.T.R.I.P.E.S. acronym reinforced what we expected of all who wore stripes in the wing--Standards, Teamwork, Responsibility, Integrity, Professionalism, Excellence in All We Do, and Service Before Self.

- Standards--Air Force Instruction 36-2618 is the solid foundation of the stripes I wear and the standard I MUST live up to. All leaders in the organization must ensure the standards are followed and the best way to do that is to set the example. Leaders are role models and live and emulate the standards.

- Teamwork--Nothing is accomplished in the organization by one individual...it takes a team. There are no Lone Rangers or Lone Wolf McQuades in the organization. Collaboration and innovation are keys to creating a successful organization.

- Responsibility--I am responsible and accountable to my Country and the Air Force to take care of the greatest national treasure, the people I lead every day. Responsibility and accountability are two key ingredients in this principle. I am responsible and I am accountable for my choices and my decisions. I am responsible for the training, coaching, mentoring, and developing the next generation of Air Force leaders. And I am accountable to my Country and the Air Force to make sure that they are ready for whenever they are called upon.

- Integrity First--Foundation of Trust and Respect in everything I do! Trust is a vital leadership asset. Trust and trustworthiness are the basis for Air Force Leaders' credibility. Integrity is a character trait. It is the willingness to do what is right even when no one is looking. It is the moral compass--the inner voice, the voice of self-control, the basis for the trust imperative in today's military.

People in the organization need to believe in their leaders. Without integrity, there is no trust in your leadership, no confidence in your actions, and your words have no meaning. There is no confidence in a leader's credibility.

- Professionalism--I am a part of the Profession of Arms and I am a Professional Warrior. Understanding that you are a part of the Profession of Arms is vital for every Airman to understand.

  Professionals are competent, qualified, proficient, and skilled experts in their field. Being part of a professional core means your character, competence, courage, and commitment are constantly focused on mission accomplishment and leading people.

- Excellence in All We Do--100% of my effort and myself--nothing less will do. Leaders have focused purpose, provide clarity to chaos, and have foresight on the direction the organization needs to go. Leaders see a person's potential even when they do not see it themselves. Leaders strive for excellence in themselves and their team. But most of all, they expect excellence in themselves and their team.

- Service Before Self--it is not about me…it is about my Country, the Air Force, and the People I serve. Leaders serve a higher purpose, to serve. People need a leader who serves because it is an honor and privilege.

    It is not about you, never has been and never will be, it is about service before self, it is about service to America, the Air Force, and the people you serve by wearing the Uniform. Leadership is not about you, it is about the team and the organization.

INSPIRE OR RETIRE

The Inspire or Retire Theorem was a declaration for all the Senior Non-Commissioned Officers in the wing to live up to the high standards and principles of Air Force leadership or to retire.

The Motto "Inspire or Retire" is a reminder to always inspire yourself and your people. As a leader, if you can no longer inspire your people, it is time to step aside and let someone else take the lead.

As a leader, you can choose to fan the flames with inspiration or you can extinguish the flames of your people. By being inspiring you can create a team of motivated people and lead your team to succeed.

THE FIRST PRINCIPLES

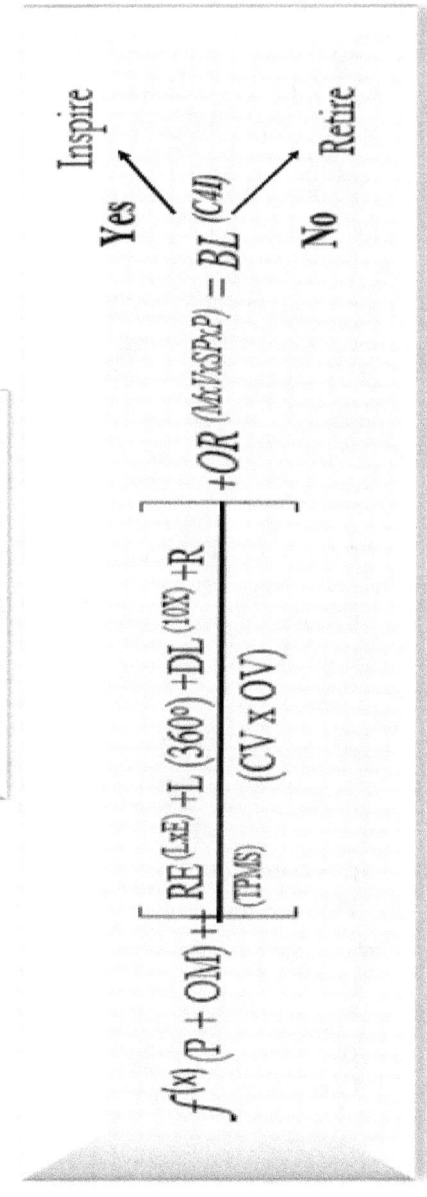

INSPIRE OR RETIRE THEOREM

$$f^{(x)}(P+OM) + \left[\frac{RE^{(LxE)} + L(360°) + DL^{(10X)} + R}{(TPMS)\ (CV \times OV)} \right] + OR^{(MxVxSPxP)} = BL^{(C4I)}$$

Yes → Inspire
No → Retire

The first part of the Theorem is a reminder that from the Junior Employee to Senior Management, leadership is everyone's business. It was designed as a visual representation for me to remember to always lead with inspiration and be people focused.

In a VUCA environment where organizations are flatter, have a networked interconnectedness leadership style, and are globally interconnected, the pace of change is exponentially faster.

$$F^{(X)} (P + OM)$$

Lead People and Execute the Mission

The Theorem further states that the overall function--the $F^{(X)}$ of every leader--is to lead and inspire People (P) and execute the Organizational Mission (OM). Since people are not things, we lead them, not manage them to lead.

$$(CV \times OV)$$

A fusion of your core values and the values of the organization

The bottom part of the equation is the fusion of your personal core values (CV) and the organization's core values (OV). This is a key and foundational organizational principle. It is the fusion or synchronization of the combined values, beliefs, and tenets of you and the organization. It is a melding of your leadership and the leadership expectations of the organization.

$$(RE^{(LxE)} + L(360°) + DL^{(10X)} + R^{(TPMS)}$$

Lead by example with 360-degree approach

As a leader of people in your organization, it is your responsibility to lead by example $RE^{(LxE)}$ and set the standard for your people. Using a 360-degree leadership approach (L (360°)), you can maximize your leadership potential by realizing that you can lead anyone, anytime, and anywhere in an organization and in your life.

To help build the organizational leadership bench in your organization and to help maximize the potential of your people, use the John Maxwell concept of developing people as leaders (DL (10X)) to increase the organizational leadership capacity by 10-fold.

Finally, as a leader, you need to build resiliency in your life and those you lead so they are well balanced and able to perform at their maximum potential. Resiliency (TPMS) (Technically, Physically, Mentally, Spiritually).

After compiling the inner equation, you need to have a holistic understanding of the Organization's (OR) Mission (M) x Vision (V) x Strategic Plan (SP) x Priorities (P) in order to develop and build leaders (BL) with Character, Competence, Courage, Commitment, and Innovation (C4I) to continue the growth and development of leaders for the organization.

$$OR^{(MxVxSPxP)} = BL^{(C4I)}$$

Understand the Organization and Build Leaders

As a leader, you need to examine yourself to see if you are inspiring your people to greater heights of performance and success. Your inspirational leadership is leading by example.

Remember, when you can no longer inspire your people to greatness and it becomes more of an effort to lead each day, then you need to move aside and allow someone else to lead.

ORGANIZATIONAL CULTURE

Leaders are the linchpin to the organization's culture and organizational effectiveness. A leader establishes the organizational culture and it begins with value alignment. In order to lead in an organization from a position of strength, you need to align your core values.

Behavior and culture must align with one another in order for change to happen. As a leader, you must make sure you do not live by two sets of values, one for yourself and one for your organization. **Bottom Line: You must be leading by example.**

Core values are an important part of organizational culture. An organizational leader must lead by example and reinforce the organizational core values daily. How successful would your team or organization be if all people in the organization aligned their core values with the organizational values? Ask yourself the following "What if" questions:

- What if everyone knew the organizational vision, goals, values, and the impact their leadership had on the success of the organization?

- What if everyone knew success as a leader included knowing themselves, their team, and the organization?

- What if everyone knew a leader must have high moral and ethical values and that character counts?

- What if everyone knew they needed to continuously develop, grow, and reinvent themselves to meet the challenges of the future?

- What if everyone knew that leaders are responsible for their actions and their words?

- What if everyone clearly understood their role in developing other organizational leaders?

- What if everyone clearly understood that character, courage, commitment, and communication are key components of leadership?

- What if everyone understood that they are responsible for their own leadership growth and development if they want to stay relevant?

This clarity of understanding how the organization works and how they fit into the overall strategy can increase their loyalty to the organization and increase productivity.

By understanding and creating an effective organizational culture, you can unleash the full potential of your leadership and your organization.

The key to organizational culture success is a top down process that engages the entire organization. Integrating the new culture and mindset into the day-to-day operation of the business helps to produce the culture shift you want to achieve.

LEADERSHIP CONGRUENCE

The words and actions of organizational leaders must be congruent to the organizational culture. A leader must walk the walk, not just talk the talk. A leader serves their people by rising above their own self-interests and embracing personal sacrifice and risk for the good of the organization and mission. An Unstoppable Leader leads by serving others.

$$Lc = \frac{Vi+S+G+O+R}{Va+B+Be+A+T}$$

The formula above is how I view leadership congruence. Leadership congruence (Lc) is a combination of your leadership capabilities and your personal capabilities. Each part of the equation must align in order for you be aligned with yourself, your team, and your organization.

The top part of the equation is your leadership Vision (Vi), your leadership Strategy (S), your Goals (G), your Objectives (O), and the Results produced from the prior parts. The bottom part of the formula are your Values (Va), your Beliefs (B), your Behavior (Be), your Attitude (A), and your Time (T).

Living your values as a leader every day is an important key component of Unstoppable Leadership. When you, your people, and your organization share a common set of values, then trust, loyalty, responsibility, and accountability increase.

Below are some suggestions for you to review and reflect on to see if you, as a leader, are living congruent to your organization.

- Evaluate and align your values with the organization so you lead from a position of strength

- Align your purpose and values with your organization's purpose and values

- Lead each day with your personal values and organization's values aligned

- Ensure leadership behavior and organizational culture is aligned

- The words and actions of organizational leaders must be congruent to the organizational culture

- A leader must walk the walk, not just talk the talk

- Reinforce organizational core values

To be successful today depends on capturing the heart, mind, body, and soul of your people. You need to align their intelligence, creative and imaginative capabilities, sense of purpose, and contributions with that of the organization. To be successful you must understand that a good team needs guidance, direction, and development to become a truly great team.

Your people deserve not only the best resources, but also the best leadership you can provide them. Your people will follow you because they believe and trust that you are acting in their best interests and not as a self-serving leader. You must set them up for success.

Bottom Line: Today, it is no longer enough for leaders or organizations to say, "People are our greatest asset." They need to back it up by recognizing that people are vital to success and that it is their capabilities, abilities, gifts, and talents that result in quantifiable outcomes and results.

COMMUNICATION IS THE KEY

A leader must have the ability to communicate effectively face-to-face. Organizations in all sectors need leaders who can communicate effectively in person and via media; who are self-disciplined and able to motivate others; and who are agile learners, able to work effectively across boundaries. Communication helps to create a culture of trust and credibility.

Your communication ability is critical to building and sustaining trust and teamwork. A leader's ability to influence comes from his or her ability to provide clear and consistent communication to their team.

LISTENING

Listening is the most neglected and underused leadership skill. Leadership is all about people and establishing relationships, and listening is important in developing, maintaining, and building lasting working relationships. Effective listening requires your attention as a leader and requires that you are physically and mentally prepared to listen. Effective listening requires an open mind in order to receive the message and to listen for ideas and themes, and not just facts.

RELATIONSHIP BUILDER

Leaders need to be masters at networking, relationships, and alliance building. A leader understands that the relationship of the leader and their team is built on trust. They use leadership influence positively and skillfully to begin action and to influence actions. They enlarge and empower all team members to work together and across functional areas.

Furthermore, a leader needs to lead across multicultural and national boundaries to increase the effectiveness of the organization. Relationship building results in both personal and professional development.

A leader needs to be able to build relationships with all people inside and outside the organization. A leader understands that a good team needs direction and growth to become a truly great team. Today more than ever it is important for leaders to be engaged with their workers.

Communication with your team is key if you want an inspired and engaged team. If a leader stays engaged with their workers, they understand they are a part of the team and the organization. Workers with engaging leaders tend to feel that their opinions count and they are important.

Communication tells your people that you consider them a key and vital member of your team and that you trust them. The lack of communication is the reason teams fail. A team leader needs to effectively communicate the strategic message of the organization and keep them informed of changes, upcoming events, and to inspire trust and respect in the group. Your people are not mushrooms, so do not leave them in the dark.

TEAM CHARTER

A team or organizational charter is a good way to align personal and organizational values and goals. The alignment of personal values and organizational values serve as a foundation for acceptable work behavior and business practices.

A charter aligns each person under the organizational purpose, mission, vision, goals, and expectations. Organizational values serve as a gauge of an organization's culture, organizational norms, and expectations. Organizations express their values and expectations through their culture.

A charter helps the team and each member to focus on the key aspects of organizational culture. It focuses their attention on cultural norms and behaviors, leader and leadership expectations, and team roles and responsibilities. Establishing a charter helps to define the organizational goals and objectives. A good start for a charter is the following:

- Create a team identity

- Clarify the team's mission

- Create and collaborate on team vision, core values, and goals

- Foster a synergy mindset by aligning organizational core values with team and personal core values

- Focus on the critical role leadership plays in achieving organizational goals and objectives

- Highlight important attributes, traits, or aspects of leadership and of each individual

- Create opportunities to improve individual innovation and creativity

- Encourage and facilitate openness and honesty within the team

- Identify opportunities for team and individual improvement, as well as problems, weaknesses, and inconsistencies in professional team development

- Provide personnel an opportunity for professional and personal leadership growth

Bottom Line: Create a collaborative and innovative team that believes in the organization and its goals.

SUMMARY

Today, the workplace is dependent on knowledge capital. As a leader, you need to keep that knowledge base in the organization and on your team. You can do that by building the relationship you have with your subordinates each day.

Lifelong learning is an individual and an organizational need. It is a constant reminder that learning is a lifelong process and is necessary to being a better leader every day.

Continuous learning provides a leader the necessary knowledge to stay current on today's trends, but also flexible and adaptive to face tomorrow's challenges. Unstoppable Leaders continuously commit to growth, development, and reinventing themselves in order to stay at the top of their game.

THE FIRST PRINCIPLES

CHARACTER CHECK

1. How well are you aligned personally and professionally?

2. How well are your values and beliefs aligned with your team and organization?

3. How congruent is your leadership?

LOOKING INTO THE MIRROR

After reading this chapter, review and reflect on the ideas and concepts presented. Think about what opportunities, challenges, resources, or blind spots you may encounter when you begin your growth and development journey.

Use the following questions to help you grow and develop.

1. How will I incorporate this principle into my leadership development?

2. What opportunity and resources exist for me to use this principle this week, this year?

3. What blind spots may derail me from using this principle?

COMMITMENT TIME

- ✓ Leading with your purpose and your core values ensures your life and leadership are congruent

- ✓ Be a role model by living out your authentic leadership daily

- ✓ Create a vision and shared purpose that people can rally around

- ✓ Stimulate and encourage creativity in your people

- ✓ Respect and celebrate each individual team member's contribution

- ✓ Provide open and honest relationships across the organization

- ✓ Build a culture that opens the door to creativity and collaboration

- ✓ Live values that connect with people's heart, mind, body, and soul

- ✓ Create open and transparent lines of communication

- ✓ Institute a leadership environment that has trust, respect, and dignity as its foundation

- ✓ Be willing to inspire or retire

LEADERSHIP NOTES

CHAPTER NINE

THE PEOPLE PRINCIPLE

BUILDING A LASTING LEADERSHIP LEGACY

"If you would not be forgotten as soon as you are dead, either write something worth reading or do something worth writing."
Benjamin Franklin

Plutarch was a Greek Philosopher and biographer who is best known for his writings called Parallel Lives and the Moralia. In his writings called *Parallel Lives*, he documents the life of the Roman General Quintus Sertorius along with several other Greek and Roman soldiers and Statesmen.

According to Plutarch, Sertorius was a military strategist and tactician, a gifted orator, and a wise leader who, because of his political alliances, left Rome and retreated to Hispania. He was a brilliant military leader who during his time in Hispania defeated armies twice his size. Quintus Sertorius, as the praetor of Hispania, had to deal with an army of undisciplined and untrained Lusitanians.

As a wise leader, he understood the value of teaching and mentoring others to increase their confidence, understanding, and ability. The lesson of two horse tails is one example of him teaching his army a lesson about the strength of perseverance and teamwork versus the brute strength of violence of a single person.

Sertorius was on the verge of battle with an army twice his size and was not pleased with the conduct and discipline of his army. His army consisted of experienced and inexperienced soldiers who, despite being hungry for battle, did not fully understand strategy and tactics and at times they were impatient, disorderly, and unruly when they were not allowed to engage the enemy.

In an effort to teach them a valuable lesson on strategy, tactics, and the strength of perseverance and persistence, he devised a lesson that would teach them. Sertorius called his armies together and then ordered two horses be brought out for all the armies to see.

The first horse was a powerful and muscular war horse with a robust and flowing tail. The second horse was an inferior and weak workhorse with a short and ragged looking tail.

Next he ordered his tallest and strongest warrior to come forward and stand next to the weak workhorse.

Then he ordered the weakest and smallest conscript to come forward and stand next to the powerful warhorse.

Sertorius then gave an order to pull the tails out of the horses. However, each individual was given different guidelines of how to pull the tail out. The strong warrior was instructed to pull the tail out all in one tuft using just his strength. The weak conscript was instructed to pull the horse hair out one by one.

The strong warrior grasped the tail and tried in vain to pull it out, but despite his strength he could not remove the tail and gave up trying. The weak conscript persevered at removing the tail because he patiently and persistently removed one strand at a time. Just like the strength of the horse's tail is in the combined strands of the tail, so is the army's strength in the combined efforts of the army, and not just each individual.

LEADERSHIP LESSONS FROM PAYPAL

I had the great fortune and opportunity to be the Keynote Speaker at PayPal's "You Are Unstoppable" Leadership Conference in Omaha, Nebraska. The conference focused on the Unstoppable potential of the men and women of PayPal.

It was a great honor to speak to over 350 PayPal Leaders at the leadership conference. However, it was an even greater honor to have the conference named after the title of my book *You Are Unstoppable*. There were several leadership lessons that came out of the conference.

First, when Linda Dugan, Vice President of PayPal Global Operations, and her leadership team interviewed me for the Keynote speaker opportunity at their Leadership Event, I asked what they wanted to accomplish and how could I help make their event a success.

During the interview, Linda and her team set some definitive goals and expectations that they wanted to accomplish for the conference. When I left the meeting, I clearly understood what they wanted to accomplish and what they expected from me.

- **Take time to set high standards and high expectations:** Make sure that you clear up all uncertainty when you are setting goals and expectations. Linda and her team clearly defined their outcomes and their vision of a successful conference. They took the time to envision the vision before they developed a clear-cut strategy to accomplish their vision. Through their single-minded focus and purpose for the conference, they set the path for a successful endeavor. Build a team that understands the vision and can accomplish it.

- **Take time to commit yourself to making an impact:** Linda and her leadership team authentically cared about and believed in the people working at PayPal. They took the time and thought necessary to create a conference that made an impact on their people. Extraordinary results happen when you take the time to give the very best you have to make an impact.

- **Be an engaged leader and understand your people and your organization:** Leadership is everyone's business. Know your people and your organization well enough to identify leadership gaps and challenges.

Second, Linda and her leadership team clearly understood that effective leadership begins at the top and permeates throughout the organization at all levels. This is a crucial factor in assuring that leadership is an organization-wide capability.

Leaders at every level in an organization must accept the responsibility to lead, take ownership of their part of the mission, and develop their people. The impact of successful leadership cascades across all departments in an organization and can affect the morale of each person. Leaders are linked to organizational culture and organizational effectiveness. Leaders who develop their people guarantee organizational success.

- **Leadership development is critical to organizational success:** Today, organizational leadership is a necessity. Every person in an organization needs to be able to lead through complexity and ambiguity. Ensure your people understand that leadership development is not an option, it is a business necessity.

People-focused leadership involves setting and clarifying organizational and developmental leadership expectations. Letting your people know what you and the organization expects of them in the area of growth and development is important. Your people need to own their leadership development and understand their importance in the organization and how you plan to invest in them.

- **Purposeful development is the key to continuous growth**: Employee growth and development are not a one-time event, they are continuous and deliberate. Therefore, it is an organizational imperative you invest in developing your people systematically and persistently. Developing leaders in a deliberate process guarantees you will produce the requisite leadership for the future. Take the time to invest in your organization and build your future leaders.

- **Your people are not just employees:** Your people are valuable assets to the growth of your organization. People enjoy coming to work with a boss who inspires them, develops them daily, and makes them feel a part of the team.

With the globalization of the world economies, the rate and pace of change, new emerging technologies, and the chaotic nature of the world today, organizations are reliant on knowledge-enabled and globally connected employees to remain competitive.

Organizations need knowledge-enabled leaders and highly competent employees.

- **Create a learning environment in which everyone can capitalize on their talents and develop their leadership:** Encourage people to expand their horizons to continuously grow, continuously develop, and continuously reinvent themselves. By growing and developing your people, you are building a leadership bench for your team and your organization. This is an organizational imperative and a necessity. These are the principles of continuous development, continuous coaching, and continuously encouraging your people.

Third and final observation, Linda and her leadership team established a level of trust, integrity, and a culture of respect in the organization. Trust is a vital component of leadership success and is the very heart of every leadership relationship.

Trust is a relationship established between you and a follower. A trustworthy leader builds a culture of integrity and respect and maintains trust with others. They interact with people unambiguously and respectfully. The relationship of the leader and the subordinate is a team relationship built on trust, respect, and integrity.

- **An authentic leader is a role model for their people:** Linda and her team took the time to make an impact on their organization and their people. Leaders must work to keep their people motivated if they plan to keep their talent. A leader who is genuine and authentic is trustworthy. Organizational leaders know talented employees stay with companies that inspire and motivate them. People want to feel a part of something that is important and will make a difference.

- **Seek to inspire trust and a higher sense of purpose:** Linda and her team sought to inspire by giving their people an opportunity to grow and develop. Inspirational leadership empowers and unleashes people's creativity, innovation, and collaboration. Trust is essential to leadership. No one wants to follow an untrustworthy leader. Trust means you are true to your word and you are an authentic leader.

- **Promote positive teamwork:** Positive teamwork supports the organization's goals and objectives and fosters behavior directed toward the achievement of theses ends. Teamwork that supports hard work, loyalty, quality consciousness, or concern for customer satisfaction are examples of positive norms. This information will communicate trust, develop responsibility, and it will reinforce the importance of growth and development to the organization.

In the end, I learned more from my time with this great organization, their great leaders, and most of all from their unstoppable people. It leaves no room for doubt as to why this organization was selected as one of the best places to work in Omaha in 2014. And it leaves no doubt that Linda Dugan and her team are leaving a legacy of inspired leaders in their wake.

LEAVING A LEGACY OF LEADERS

"Our chief want is someone who will inspire us to be what we know we could be."
Ralph Waldo Emerson

The true measure of your success as a leader is not the corner office, not the accolades for your accomplishments, or the promotions. These are the benefits of success, they are not your true legacy.

Your true measure of success and your leadership legacy are the people you helped to grow, develop, and become leaders in their own right. Your true legacy is the investment you made to mentor, coach, and teach others by being a servant leader.

Unstoppable Leaders develop their replacements and look for talent, skills, and potential in their people. This is important because each person has different goals, ideas, skills, and leadership potential. A leader must be flexible and adaptive to quickly respond to crisis and to change. A leader must maintain organizational effectiveness during major changes in work tasks or work environment.

As a leader you have an opportunity to make an impact on your organization and your people. A great leader understands that any achievements they achieve are due to the people of the team they lead.

Unstoppable Leaders serve their people by rising above their own self-interests and embracing personal sacrifice and risk for the good of the organization and mission. A great leader is always looking out for their people's best interest. A leader is a visionary person who inspires others to follow their lead and has the capability to make everyone in the organization feel unique.

A successful leader uses a broad brush and paints the strategic picture for their people. Through this strategic painting, the leader charts the course for everyone to follow and captures the heart of the people. People enjoy coming to work with a boss who inspires them, develops them daily, and makes them feel a part of the team.

EVERY PERSON IS A POTENTIAL LEADER

Today, the real key to leadership is leading with your people. People are looking for leaders who inspire them. They are looking for meaning and purpose, not trophies and awards. When authentic leaders inspire people, they reach new levels of innovation, achievement, and commitment.

Each person in your organization is a potential leader, emerging leader, or an enduring leader, so they must be developed based on where they are in their development.

Avoid the cookie cutter approach or the "one size fits all" approach when developing your people. Establish individualized learning plans for all participants based on individualized assessment.

Developing each person at their level of readiness will ensure that people are developed at their level of competence. It will ensure that the leadership pipeline always has bench strength of developing leaders for the organization.

EVERY LEADER MUST MENTOR

You need to equip your senior leaders to be teachers, coaches, and mentors for the potential and emerging leaders. You have invested a great deal of capital in their development, so it is time they give back to the organization to help it grow the next generation of leaders.

As a leader of other leaders, you need to create a leadership-centered culture that contributes to a foundation of trust and mutual respect, which drives greater mission success. Another important aspect is to create and sustain an organizational culture conducive to learning and development so that leadership can flourish and prosper.

TAKE TIME TO BUILD THE FUTURE

To leave a legacy of leaders in your wake you need to be a teacher, coach, and mentor to the people you lead each day. Your greatest contribution to your team and your organization is leaving qualified leaders to replace you when you ae promoted, leave the organization, or retire. Building future leaders only occurs with decisive and purposeful action on the part of the leader to establish an authentic relationship with their people in order to grow and develop them.

As teacher, coach, and mentor you need to build up employee commitment and confidence to drive greater performance. You need to develop individual skills, talents, and abilities to grow the next generation of leaders.

Finally, you inspire and guide others by sharing your knowledge, experiences, and wisdom to shape and mold the individual to help them achieve their goals.

Teach: The principal purpose of a teacher is to educate and to transfer information and bestow knowledge on the apprentice or trainee. As the teacher, you need to teach the skills, knowledge, and aptitudes essential to accomplish the job successfully.

Your role as the teacher means that you outline the fundamentals parts of the task to perform and to impart the information to the trainee.

Provide step-by-step instructions that involves your trainee in doing the tasks or procedures. On-the-job training is your most effective teaching tool.

Coach: The principal purpose of a coach is to sharpen career and leadership skills and give direction on how to improve those skills. Your role is to challenge your employee to execute to the best of their ability and as independently as possible. As the coach, you help your employee to develop professional and leadership expertise and set realistic and achievable goals.

You encourage and provide the necessary leadership to grow and develop the apprentice for the mission today, but also to face the challenges of the future. Coaching helps you grow a junior employee into a productive member of the team and sets them up for future success.

Mentor: The name mentor is derived from Homer's epic poem the Odyssey. Mentor, an old friend of King Odysseus, is left in charge of the King's son, Telemachus, when he goes to fight the Trojan wars. Through the teaching of Mentor, Telemachus grows to Manhood and assists his father in reclaiming his kingdom.

Mentoring focuses on developing the whole person and is a collaborative relationship in which a leader with more experience and knowledge mentors another person. A mentor is one who is willing to share their skills, knowledge, and expertise to grow and develop another person.

Develop your people through constant dialogue and feedback. Feedback is a mechanism we use to share information on performance, learning, and goal achievement.

Dialogue is more of a human interaction method of sharing information, ideas, points of view, and connecting at the human level versus professional level.

Dialogue helps build trust, respect, and lets your people know you care about them as people and not just workers.

NO PEOPLE--NO LEADERSHIP

In December 2006, I had the unique opportunity to travel with Multi-National Force-Iraq Command Sergeant Major Jeff Mellinger, 5th Fleet Command Master Chief Kelly Schneider, and several other senior enlisted to visit the U.S.S. Dwight D. Eisenhower in the Arabian Gulf. We flew out of Bahrain and landed on the Nimitz-class aircraft carrier 3.5 hours later.

The visit had several planned events to see the sailors and aircraft in action--day and night flight deck operations, aircraft maintenance operations, tours of the combat direction center and bridge, and to have morning physical therapy in one of the main hangar bays looking out at the ocean.

The main purpose of the visit provided an opportunity to connect and interact with the sailors and let them know how they were contributing to the troops on the ground and to get to know them--who they are, why they joined, and about their future plans.

It helped us, as senior leaders, to connect "down to the deck plates" with the sailors and allowed us to tell their stories when we got back to each of our respective units. The visit created an opportunity to bridge gaps in our learning and leadership by understanding a more strategic leadership landscape from the tactical edge.

It reminded us that leadership is all about people; therefore, all leadership is relational. As a leader, part of your daily mission is to grow and develop your people. Your goal is to help them grow and develop as leaders in your organization in the same way you are developing.

A leader who invests the time and patience to grow an emerging leader into an enduring leader reaps the benefit of increased organizational leadership capacity.

Leading and developing others is a key part of Unstoppable Leadership. It requires that you take the time and attention to detail to know your people. You are accountable and responsible for your people and the success of your team.

Today, more than ever, it is important for leaders to be engaged with their people. If a leader stays engaged with their people, they understand they are a part of the team and the organization. People with engaging leaders tend to feel that their opinions count and they are important.

SUMMARY

An Unstoppable Leader's success comes not from their own individual strength, skills, talents, or abilities. It comes from their ability to communicate an inspiring vision, establishing attainable team goals, and then using the combined strength of the team to pull together in the direction of the vision, goals, and outcomes.

The one takeaway that you can learn from the leaders in your life is as a leader you have an opportunity to make an impact on your organization and your people. You need to demonstrate respect and trust for the individual you are developing personally, professionally, and in their leadership role.

As a mentor, you are a role model for the individual to emulate. You need to be a living example of the values, ethics, leadership, and professional principles that you want the individual to inculcate.

CHARACTER CHECK

1. What will be your Leadership Legacy?

2. Who is your replacement?

3. How are you serving your people?

4. How well do you encourage and inspire?

LOOKING INTO THE MIRROR

After reading this chapter, review and reflect on the ideas and concepts presented. Think about what opportunities, challenges, resources, or blind spots you may encounter when you begin your growth and development journey.

Use the following questions to help you grow and develop.

1. How will I incorporate this principle into my leadership development?

2. What opportunity and resources exist for me to use this principle this week, this year?

3. What blind spots may derail me from using this principle?

THE FIRST PRINCIPLES

COMMITMENT TIME

- ✓ Lead by inspiring your people each day
- ✓ Lead by encouraging and developing your people daily
- ✓ Lead by serving
- ✓ Lead by teaching, mentoring, and coaching your people
- ✓ Lead by being fully engaged with your team and organization
- ✓ Lead by recognizing the potential and possibilities of your people
- ✓ Inspire and guide your people by sharing your knowledge, experiences, and wisdom to shape and mold the individual to help them achieve their goals
- ✓ Building leaders assists others in their development and allows you to be a servant leader by helping them grow
- ✓ Leave a legacy of leaders in your path
- ✓ Create opportunities to improve your people's leadership capacity and capability

THE FIRST PRINCIPLES

LEADERSHIP NOTES

CONCLUSION

"If your actions inspire others to dream more, learn more, do more and become more, you are a leader."
John Quincy Adams

A good friend asked me if I enjoyed my tenure as the United States Strategic Command Senior Enlisted Leader. Without hesitation I answered with a resounding YES!! I went on to add that the opportunity to serve at the Combatant Command level was an honor and a privilege to advance a greater good and serve a higher cause.

It also opened my eyes to how the Department of Defense operated at the strategic, operational, and the tactical levels of war, and how each Service brings its unique war fighting capabilities to bear to make the vicious harmony of warfare happen.

I also had the opportunity to meet and coin the outstanding men and women across the command. I further broke it down into three main areas that I felt targeted what leadership opportunities it provided.

First, as a Combatant Command Senior Enlisted Leader, I had the opportunity to serve our Nation and understand the scope, depth, and breadth of USSTRATCOM's global enterprise. I also had the unique opportunity of not only understanding how each Service operated within a joint, multinational, and multiagency environment, but also to see it happen on a daily basis.

Daily in our Headquarters and throughout my travels to our Joint Functional Component Commands and Service Component units, I have watched our men and women operate alongside each other, our allies, and our coalition partners.

Second, operating at the Combatant Command level meant that I built strategic partnerships and alliances with each of the fifty-four Service Components, Joint Functional Component Commands, and our Nuclear Task Force Senior Enlisted Leaders assigned to USSTRATCOM. A critical requirement in my job was to build a senior enlisted strategic leadership team by building trust, creating a common understanding of our joint missions, and by working closely with each Senior Enlisted Leader.

This strategic leadership team's mission was to provide leadership across the USSTRATCOM global enterprise. They looked for solutions to problems and challenges that the force was facing, and to make sure every person assigned or attached to USSTRATCOM believed in our mission, was committed to the mission, and owned the mission.

Third, operating at the Combatant Command level meant that I traveled quite extensively, logging over 50 thousand miles and spending 391 days on the road to see and meet our enlisted Soldiers, Sailors, Airmen, and Marines attached and or assigned to USSTRATCOM. It was during my trips that I had the opportunity to get to know, listen to, and to understand our enlisted corps.

I took the time to see the places they operated in, how they executed their operational missions, and to have dinner with them and their families. It was important for me to understand and get to know our people and find out how I could serve them better; being a Servant Leader was critically important to me.

I served in the Air Force as a Sergeant through Chief Master Sergeant for 24.5 years of my 28 years. The years serving in the capacity of sergeant defined my purpose and shaped my servant leader outlook and leadership competence. To me, leading is synonymous with serving.

When you break down the word sergeant, it means to serve. The Latin etymology for the word "sergeant" is serviens, meaning "serving." If you use the present active, servio means, "I serve." Therefore, when I retired from the military as Chief Master Sergeant, I retired as a Chief Master Servant. My role was to be a "servant leader who grows the next generation of leaders."

My purpose in life is to serve and develop other people. It is something I have had a passion for throughout the last 28 years. This may sound pedestrian, but it is true. My purpose gave me direction, focus, and energy to develop and grow my replacements. My life's purpose defined my life and my career. Even when I retired, my passion for developing my replacements was still a major concern.

Leaders best serve their people and organization by understanding and knowing their people's aspirations, goals, and dreams, and best aligning them with the organizational needs.

A leader must develop trust and understanding with and among them. I have always regarded that the true essence of leadership is about serving others. It is about putting the needs of your people and your team before your own self-interests. One of the Air Force Core Values that shaped me as a leader was Service Before Self.

For me, servant leadership is a lifestyle and a way of life and not just a saying. Being a servant leader allowed me to not only ensure the mission was accomplished, but to help my people grow, develop, and become servant leaders in their own right.

An Unstoppable Leader is only as good as the personal example they demonstrate. Living and Leading by example is fundamental to Unstoppable Leadership. Everything you do as an Unstoppable Leader should be authentic and congruent. Your actions, behaviors, and words should align with your core values, beliefs, and worldview.

By taking responsibility and demanding accountability of yourself, you set an example for your people to follow. Your people will perform to the standard you set for yourself and the organization. Truly effective leaders are those who have figured out what is important to them, what matters in their life, and what they stand for. They have identified their purpose and are living it daily.

Unstoppable Leaders passionately pursue their purpose in life and relentlessly challenge themselves to become better. Few things are more important to a leader than a vision for their life and a mission statement to achieve that vision.

- Lead with purpose and passion

- Establish and sustain trust, credibility, and trustworthiness

- Learn to lead across all three areas of leadership: Tactical, Operational, and Strategic

YOUR LIFE IS YOUR MESSAGE

Each day you live, you write a page in your life story. Each year you live, you add another chapter to your life story. Everything you say and do in your life adds to your life story. Your life story is your message to the world. What will your life story say about you? What will your message tell the world?

Will your message tell of a great odyssey like Odysseus had or will it tell a great tale of overcoming the odds like Earnest Shackleton? Will your message tell the world you lived an Unstoppable Life or will it tell a tale of mediocrity and a tale of an unlived life?

The truth is that you get to choose what your message will say because you get to write the storyline. Maybe you have been living uneventfully and maybe the message is not telling the story you want the world to read and hear. If that is true, then you can choose TODAY to write a new page in your Unstoppable Life.

Stop for a moment and think about what you want your life to become. Think about what you want your message to be. Think about the difference, the significance, the impact, and the inspiration your message can bring to others. What will your life message say to the world?

Almost every minute of your life there is an opportunity to choose your response to life. Do you choose to proactively respond to life, negatively respond to life, or just react to whatever challenges life throws at you?

Your learning experiences arise from day-to-day activities, from moving out of your comfort zone and through your trials and challenges. Do not run from your problems or challenges, face them head on and tackle them. You need to tackle them as soon as they happen.

Life is not easy. It will try to define you, especially when you plan to achieve success. Push back, forge ahead, and create greatness. You need to maintain a positive perspective as you grow from your challenges.

If you want to be unstoppable, you need to concentrate on the positives in every situation. Take risks in your leadership. You will stumble and fail at times. In addition, when you do stumble, get up, dust yourself off, and press forward with your life. A critical component of leadership is pressing forward and reviewing what your challenges have taught you.

THE EIGHT KEYS

"All we have to decide is what to do with the time that is given us."
J. R. R. Tolkien

The key to understanding how to lead is to know who you are as a person first. What do you believe in? What do you value? What motivates you? An understanding of your personal strengths and weaknesses allows you to make your leadership more effective. Knowing yourself makes you more effective in your organization, with teams, and with others.

Each day you choose to operate in your unstoppable nature or you choose to operate out of your mediocre nature. The choice is made when you decide to proactively create your day or just live in the day and accept whatever comes your way. It is a choice of desire and fire or a choice of complacency and just good enough. Living an unstoppable life is a choice and you must make the choice to be unstoppable.

Throughout my life and leadership, I found eight keys to living an Unstoppable Life and building an Unstoppable Leadership lifestyle.

FIRST KEY--BE INSPIRED

To live an Unstoppable Life you need to live inspired and live for more than just yourself. When you live an Unstoppable Life you are an inspiration to others. On October 3, 1889, General Joshua L. Chamberlain said these inspiring words at the dedication of the Maine Monuments at Gettysburg Battlefield Cemetery:

> The inspiration of a noble cause involving human interests wide and far, enables men to do things they did not dream themselves capable of before, and which they were not capable of alone. The consciousness of belonging, vitally, to something beyond individuality; of being part of a personality that reaches we know not where, in space and time, greatens the heart to the limits of the soul's ideal, and builds out the supreme of character. In great deeds, something abides.
>
> On great fields something stays. Forms change and pass; bodies disappear; but spirits linger, to consecrate the ground for the vision-place of souls. And reverent men and women from afar, and generations that know us not and that we know not of, heart-drawn to see where and by whom great things were suffered and done for them, shall come to this deathless field, to ponder and dream; and lo! the shadow of a mighty presence shall wrap them in its bosom, and the power of the vision pass into their

souls. This is the great reward of service, to live, far out and on, in the life of others.

Chamberlain was talking about the reward of service before self, in the ability to live your life–far beyond your own life–through service to others as an inspiration. Truly effective leaders are those who have figured out what is important to them, what matters in their life, and what they stand for. They have identified their purpose and are living it daily.

Unstoppable Leaders passionately pursue their purpose in life and relentlessly challenge themselves to become better. Few things are more important to a leader than a vision for their life and a mission statement to achieve that vision.

- Lead with purpose and passion

- Establish and sustain trust, credibility, and trustworthiness

- Learn to lead across all three areas of leadership: Tactical, Operational, and Strategic

SECOND KEY--LIVE GREATLY

To live an Unstoppable Life, you need to live greatly and not a life of mediocrity. Living greatly means you live a life that counts and live it abundantly. On April 23, 1910, President Teddy Roosevelt spoke these words at the Sorbonne in Paris, France:

THE FIRST PRINCIPLES

> It is not the critic who counts; not the man who points out how the strong man stumbles, or where the doer of deeds could have done them better. The credit belongs to the man who is actually in the arena, whose face is marred by dust and sweat and blood; who strives valiantly; who errs, who comes short again and again, because there is no effort without error and shortcoming; but who does actually strive to do the deeds; who knows great enthusiasms, the great devotions; who spends himself in a worthy cause; who at the best knows in the end the triumph of high achievement, and who at the worst, if he fails, at least fails while daring greatly, so that his place shall never be with those cold and timid souls who neither know victory nor defeat.

What he was talking about was living greatly and persevering throughout your life. Teddy Roosevelt was an example of living an Unstoppable Life. When he was young, he suffered from asthma and other childhood sicknesses that could have left him weak and fragile throughout his early life.

He challenged himself daily, developed his mind and body, and put himself in situations, which required him to grow in order to overcome what life had put upon him. He challenged himself to live a life of greatness and abundance instead of a life of mediocrity.

Life is not easy. It will try to define you, especially when you plan to achieve success. Push back, forge ahead, and create greatness. You need to maintain a positive perspective as you grow from your challenges. If you want to be unstoppable, you need to concentrate on the positives and look for the positive aspect in every situation.

THIRD KEY--CHANGE YOURSELF

To live an Unstoppable Life you need to change yourself every year and develop a life development plan. At the beginning of each new day, take the opportunity to start a portion of your life over by establishing new goals and new opportunities to change your life. Change is not easy and takes some perseverance and willpower. Anything is possible if you are determined to make it.

Take risks in your leadership; you will stumble and fail at times. When you do stumble, get up, dust yourself off, and press forward with your life. A critical component of leadership is pressing forward and reviewing what your challenges have taught you. You must learn each day to be an Unstoppable Leader.

FOURTH KEY--CHANGE YOUR MINDSET

Being unstoppable is a mindset. It is an unwavering belief in yourself, your abilities, and your capabilities. It is a belief in your unshakeable purpose and values. You have to believe in yourself with conviction and commitment. It is an awareness of your strengths and your challenges. It is about self-efficacy, self-awareness, and intentional clarity.

Once you have recognized your purpose and values and ingrained them, you begin to shape your Unstoppable Life. Unless you have an unwavering belief that you have something of value to offer this world you'll never be unstoppable.

The unstoppable mindset means that no matter what life tosses in your way, you can overcome it. It is about being fearless. Fear is a creation of your mind. It is a response to an uncertainty or an unknown. You need to be fearless in your life to be unstoppable.

Being fearless is overcoming your feelings of fear and pushing through the uncertainty. The only way to combat fear is to face your fear and take the necessary action to alleviate it. To get over fear, you have to take action. Being unstoppable is about making life choices.

Life is a series of choices, and every choice you make defines you. The most important choice you can make is who you will become. If you want to live an Unstoppable Life, you need to change your mindset and win the war of your thinking. You have tremendous inner strength as an individual and by applying this inner strength, you can achieve what you want in life. By changing the way you think and applying different effects in your life, you can create new possibilities in your life.

FIFTH KEY--TAKE CHARGE OF YOUR LIFE

The true key, if you want to live an Unstoppable Life, is to take 100% control of your life. Stop blaming others for your failures and faults and start accepting responsibility for your life. If you want to succeed in life, you need to create the outcomes of your life and quit letting others dictate your life.

You are the owner of your success, failures, emotions, and feelings. So, take ownership of your life! To be truly unstoppable you must take charge of your life. As long as you are bound to others for their acceptance and approval, you will not own your life.

Living an Unstoppable Life is the freedom and liberty to express yourself authentically and unapologetically. If you are consumed by the need for others to accept you, then you will be consumed trying to prove that you are worthy of their approval.

You need to realize that you are worthy and loved in your own right without others justifying your existence. You need to have the courage to be yourself and accept who you are and what you have to offer the world.

SIXTH KEY--YOU ARE RESPONSIBLE

To begin taking ownership of your life, you need to realize that you are given 24 hours each day to use as you wish--24 hours, no more no less; not a minute more. You can choose to use that time to create or change your life's outcomes, or you can chose to waste the hours. The choice is yours.

How you choose to use the hours will determine if you will be successful or if you are wasting your time on earth. Each day, each hour, each minute is a gift of life and opportunity. You need to unwrap each day as a gift and see what you can do with the gift to make your life unstoppable!

If you want to be successful, if you want to "be alive," if you want to have great passion for living on purpose, then you need to take responsibility for all aspects of your life--successes and failures. They are yours, you own them. Be intentional about your purpose in life.

Your thoughts, attitude, choices, and your decisions are the reason you are where you are today. Your life is the outcome of how you look at life, your attitude toward life, your choices, and decisions you make in life.

You are the sum of these four. You are free to shape your attitude, free to change your thoughts, and free to make life choices and life decisions, but you must also understand the second, third, and fourth order of effects/consequences of these four areas.

SEVENTH KEY--YOU ARE ACCOUNTABLE

You are accountable for how you make your choices in life, how well you prepare yourself in life, and how you persevere and persist against the odds; but moreover, you are accountable for your outlook or attitude about your life.

You need to own your decisions, choices, and mistakes and be ready and willing to take the essential steps to learn from them. You must take accountability for your life or someone else will. Where you are today in this moment of time is a direct result of your choices and decisions. But, where you go in the future depends on what you envision for your life and what actions you plan to take to make it happen.

EIGHTH KEY--NEVER GIVE UP

To live an Unstoppable Life you must never give up on yourself, your dreams, or your life vision. You must never give up on believing in yourself, who you are, and what you are capable of doing. You must not give up on yourself, your dreams, or your desire to be unstoppable. You can choose to live a mediocre life or you can choose to push back on life and live a life of significance and impact. Seek to be the very best person you can become each day.

The degree to which you can realize your dreams is contingent on you taking responsibility and never giving up on your life. No one can live your life or make your decisions. Living an Unstoppable Life is a choice and you must make the choice to be unstoppable.

No one else is responsible for your life or cares about your life as much you do. You must take responsibility for your life, believe in your possibilities, and look for your opportunities.

You must change your mindset, see yourself as unstoppable, and live inspired each day. You will learn more from your mistakes, errors, and challenges than you will learn from your successes.

BE AN UNSTOPPABLE LEADER NOW!

Life and Leadership are treks of trials, challenges, experiences, setbacks, and successes. It is a time of choices, responses, outcomes, and decisions. It is a time of soul-searching, self-discovery, and developing a new understanding of who you are and what you are capable of doing in life.

Leadership is a time of opportunities, possibilities, learning, and development. It is also a time of adventure, misfortune, victory, and defeat. How you travel along your life's journey is up to you. However, on each leadership expedition you have the opportunity to grow, develop, and reinvent yourself.

You need to convert all your leadership expedition experiences into life lessons and leverage those lessons into how you live and lead each day. The key is to live each day in the same manner you want to finish life. You can live an Unstoppable Life and lead well each day by choosing to be an Unstoppable Leader now!

- The best way to live an Unstoppable Life is to prepare and plan your life NOW!

- The best way to live out your Unstoppable Life and be an Unstoppable Leader is through your passion for life and day-to-day performance!

Start your Leadership Expedition today!

THE FIRST PRINCIPLES

LEADERSHIP NOTES

L.I.F.E. BOOKS

I developed the L.I.F.E. book series to encapsulate my passion for developing people and helping them to live their lives to their utmost. The acronym L.I.F.E. stands for Leadership, Inspiration, Faith, and Empowerment. The philosophy behind L.I.F.E. books is detailed on the following pages:

Leadership

I am passionate about developing emerging, enduring, and experienced leaders and teaching them how to develop themselves using a disciplined and deliberate approach. All leadership begins from inside a person and must be developed and grown as they grow into emerging and enduring leaders.

Leadership starts with a condition of your heart--it is the desire and the passion to make a difference before it moves to your brain to implement an action plan to make a difference. Before you can make an impact on the world, you must first make an impact on yourself by discovering your purpose, your values, and by knowing who you are.

Inspiration

Inspiration is the ability to breathe life into your life and others. Inspiration is a positive influence and a positive reinforcement of life. It ignites desire, ignites creativity, and ignites innovation in inspired people. Your life's purpose is your daily inspiration for living abundantly. Your purpose excites you, energizes you, and fills you with a great sense of drive and determination.

Faith

Your faith provides you focus and vision for your life. It is your true north compass and GPS of self-awareness and self-management. Your faith is your lens to focus on how your talents, skills, gifts, and abilities will allow you to live on purpose. By focusing each day you can remove the noise and clutter of life to achieve your life's purpose. Living your faith daily matters immeasurably in everything you do. The better you pay attention to your life and faith, the greater your life outcomes. Your faith helps you to focus on your life choices, life opportunities, and life possibilities.

Empowerment

It is your life...**OWN IT!** Your life purpose empowers you and enables you to live life abundantly. Empowerment begins by taking responsibility for your life and being accountable for your actions. Empowerment is the courage to live passionately and purposefully each day. Anything is possible when you choose to believe in yourself, your life's purpose, and your talents, skills, and abilities. Your life purpose unleashes you to live your life and allows you to be unstoppable.

L.I.F.E. BOOKS

"The significant problems we face cannot be solved at the same level of thinking we were at when we created them."
Albert Einstein

F(X) Leadership Unleashed! is a different kind of leadership development book. It is a comprehensive leadership development approach hitting all the areas and aspects of creating great leaders, starting with yourself first. It combines the Art and the Science of leadership. It encompasses tried and proven leadership concepts in a way that is easily charted throughout all levels of an organization because it provides a roadmap and the compass.

F(X) Leadership Unleashed! will benefit anyone who seeks to inspire, impact, ignite or lead others, whether they are military, civilian, corporate or community leaders.

This book is about you and your journey to be the best person and leader that you are meant to be. It's intended to help you discover and identify who you are and why you are here.

This book is designed to make you think about your life and how you are developing yourself and living your life. Your life is a sum total of the decisions, choices, and actions you have taken so far in your life. However, in reality it is only a sliver of what is in the realm of possibility for your life. Hidden deep within you is an unstoppable life waiting to emerge. You are an unstoppable person, wonderfully made, and born to thrive each day, not merely survive.

However, if you are like most skeptical people and you do not completely grab hold of this concept, then this book will challenge you to look at your life and how you are developing yourself. Even if you do not believe it yet, **I believe that You Are Unstoppable!**

ABOUT THE AUTHOR

Thomas S. Narofsky is the Founder and Chief Inspirational Officer for the Narofsky Consulting Group and is the author of *F(X) Leadership Unleashed: The Art and Science of Leadership* and *You Are Unstoppable: Unleash Your Inspired Life!*

Thom served as the third Command Senior Enlisted Leader for United States Strategic Command and oversaw the enlisted professional development programs, military readiness, and mission effectiveness of 35,000 men and women. He has led men and women during combat, crisis, and peace.

As one of the Top 15 Senior Enlisted Leaders in the Department of Defense, he served on the Department of Defense Senior Enlisted Leader Council, the United States Strategic Command Joint Enlisted Development Council, and the United States Air Force Enlisted Board of Directors. He was responsible for developing long-range plans, teaching concepts, and a disciplined approach for delivery of professional and leadership development to produce skilled, knowledgeable, and adaptive leaders.

Thom has traveled the world teaching professional and leadership development seminars for American, Korean, Japanese, Australian, British, Canadian, Belgian, and German enlisted forces. He retired on November 1, 2011 after serving 28 years on active duty in the United States Air Force. His military decorations include the Defense Superior Service medal and Bronze Star medal.

Thom is an adjunct professor at Bellevue University, a USSTRATCOM senior mentor for the National Defense University KEYSTONE Leadership Development Program, and is a graduate of the National Defense University and Joint Staff College Joint Senior Leader Professional Military Education Courses.

Thom is a Doctoral Candidate in Business Administration with a specialization in Leadership at Capella University and currently holds a Master of Arts in Leadership, a Master of Science in Information Technology Management, and has Executive Leadership Development Certificates from the Center for Creative Leadership, University of North Carolina at Chapel Hill, and the University of Tennessee.

www.ingramcontent.com/pod-product-compliance
Lightning Source LLC
Chambersburg PA
CBHW051631170526
45167CB00001B/141